WHAT'S WRONG WITH US?

WHAT'S WRONG WITH US?

A Coach's Blunt Take on the State of American Soccer After a Lifetime on the Touchline

BRUCE ARENA

WITH STEVE KETTMANN

HARPER

An Imprint of HarperCollins*Publishers*

HarperCollins books may be purchased for educational, business, or sales
promotional use. For information, please email the Special Markets Department at SPsales@harpercollins.com.

FIRST EDITION

Soccer ball image by Sergey Peterman/Shutterstock, Inc.

Library of Congress Cataloging-in-Publication Data has been applied for.

ISBN 978-0-06-280394-8

18 19 20 21 22   LSC   10 9 8 7 6 5 4 3 2 1

To my wife, Phyllis; and my son, Kenny;
my daughter-in-law, Jenny; and my grandchildren,
Wayde and Holden; and to my parents and
brothers and sister. I love you guys.

Contents

Introduction:
Time for Long-Overdue Changes

Most coaches learn sooner or later that you live or die with your last result. I was on the sideline for some of the best moments in the history of US soccer, like when we beat Mexico to advance to play Germany in the quarterfinals of the 2002 World Cup in South Korea and Japan. That was as far as a US side has ever advanced in the world's greatest sporting event, and really, I thought we outplayed Germany that day. I was also on the sideline for one of the low points in the history of US soccer, our shocking loss to Trinidad and Tobago in October 2017. That 2–1 defeat meant that we failed to qualify for the 2018 World Cup in Russia, something the United States had done every four years going back to 1986. We failed that day, and I failed in my mission to pick up the pieces when I was hired in the middle of the qualifying process. I knew when I took the job, in late November 2016, that we had a steep road ahead of us if we were going to pull it off, but if I had it all to do over again, I'd take the job again in a second. Even though people don't want to hear it, I don't think that, given the limited time I had, there is much I would do differently, either.

I felt terrible after the Trinidad loss, as I think everyone in US soccer did. What bothered me the most wasn't the usual Monday-morning quarterbacking and self-righteous indignation, some of it directed at US soccer in general, much of it aimed at me personally. You expect that stuff; there's value in some of it, and you just tune out the rest. What made me sick was the knowledge that our players would all be denied the experience of playing for their country in Russia on the greatest stage in sport. The World Cup in Russia could have been and should have been the true coming-out party for our young star Christian Pulisic, who, as I said on a CBS *60 Minutes* segment, just might be our first true American soccer superstar. Christian was the best player for us in World Cup qualifying and continued to develop at an impressive rate. In 2018 in Russia, he would have been a player to watch. I felt so bad knowing Christian would be denied that. Veteran players like Tim Howard and Clint Dempsey, huge figures in bringing US soccer forward, would have to sit out the World Cup too, along with our team captain, Michael Bradley, along with every member of the squad. A lot of these guys will never get another shot at a World Cup and that might even include Michael, who was one of our better players in qualifying behind Christian—he'll be thirty-five by the time the 2022 World Cup in Qatar rolls around, and that might be pushing it. I also felt terrible for soccer fans in this country. We usually have one of the largest group of supporters at the World Cup, and missing out was a real blow to them.

But there are also positives. For a start, the devastating result forces a wholesale evaluation of the state of soccer in this country, and it has been much needed for a while. I hope that this book will be seen as part of the process by which we work out what went wrong and what we need to do to fix the problems. We've come so far since I first started coaching soccer more than forty years ago, and I hope in these pages to tell enough stories and share enough experiences from those forty years to give a sense of just how far soccer *has* come in this country—and how honored I've been to have played a role in that progress. One example is the fact that millions of Americans, including me, cared enough about soccer to feel pained that our great country will not be represented in Russia.

One of the key problems with soccer in the United States right now is the inability to make a distinction between making money and developing the sport. We've pretended that the two goals are the same, when in fact they're only somewhat related. For years the challenge seemed to be to find a way to have a viable North American professional soccer league, which was rightly seen as the foundation for continuing to move soccer forward in the United States. People were understandably haunted by the memory of the North American Soccer League, launched in 1968 and featuring the likes of Pelé and Franz Beckenbauer (and, if I'd agreed to a contract, a young backup goalkeeper named Bruce Arena), a league that drew millions of fans but which ultimately folded in 1984. Fast forward to Major League Soccer, which was founded in 1996, and which found itself in financial trouble as early as 1999. That was the year when MLS hired as its commissioner Don Garber, whose background was in NFL marketing, not soccer.

Don has done a good job running Major League Soccer as a business. The league keeps expanding, it's on firm financial footing, many clubs have built fine, soccer-only stadiums, and fans around the country can look forward to a steadily improving level of play. My 1997 and 1998 DC United teams were as good as any teams in the history of the league, but overall the level of play is clearly better—and will continue to improve.

The question is: are we headed in the right direction? Is the sole purpose of MLS to make money, to build itself into a fabulous sports business like the NFL, or is it also to provide the foundation for the United States to build itself into a true world soccer power? I think most fans of US soccer would see it as both. It's time to do far more to give young players a way forward, not just at the youth level, but at the young professional level. The whole relationship between the United States Soccer Federation

(US Soccer for short) and Major League Soccer needs to be re-worked and rethought.

By the time you read these words, the US Soccer Federation will have a new president, but I'm afraid I have to say that both US Soccer and Major League Soccer need leadership that is more focused on the sport. It's great to establish a strong financial footing, and MLS has done that, but the decision makers at both the federation and MLS need to become much more acquainted with the technical side of the sport, that is, the sport of soccer itself, not soccer just as a business.

If you want to be successful on the field of play, that needs to carry over into every decision you make. Every single thing you do should be done with an eye on how to give your team—or sport—an edge. If that means hosting a World Cup qualifying game against Mexico in Alaska, then maybe you give that some thought. It makes me think of something David Beckham said for this book. "All great players need a ruthless streak that runs through their veins, and all great managers need that—and that's what Bruce has as well," he said. He's right! To build a championship team you have to have an edge, an intensity, that may rub some people the wrong way; you're not always going to win friends, but people will respect you for it. Our soccer leadership in this country needs more of an edge. It needs to be on a mission, focused on making the hard choices that help get our sport over the top competitively.

After our setback in Trinidad, I was accused of not talking enough about the fact that the sky was falling. I called the loss a "blemish," which didn't go over well. I think people wanted to see me weeping or screaming. Believe me, I felt like it, but you know what else I was feeling? A sense of: *Welcome to my world!* Soccer in our country has had major issues for years. If we had equalized in the second half in Trinidad, gotten our one point and then moved on to the World Cup, no one would have been focused on those issues—they'd have been swept under the rug again. We were in a precarious position all through qualifying, and that caught up with us. Blame is not the issue. I'm more than comfortable taking the fall for failing to qualify for the World Cup. But who really cares about blame? We should care about the future. We should care about making real progress toward fielding a very competitive team in the World Cup that can rise to the challenge to hold up that trophy.

The first enemy is complacency. We've been sitting around like fat cats thinking we deserve to go to every World Cup. That was always a mistake. So if for some people failure to qualify was a wakeup call, and they're now on board with the need for change, that's great. I was already awake—I didn't need a call. The chance to participate in a World Cup for a country is a privilege, and it needs to be earned. All around the world, we witness a very competitive World Cup qualifying cycle. For example, when a country with the tradition of Argentina has to qualify in 2017 on the last day of the competition off the magic of Lionel Messi, it should tell you something. And how about the fact that four-time World Cup champion Italy didn't qualify for Russia? Or that the Netherlands, with their great player-development model, didn't make it either?

The next issue to face is that we have to keep up with the teams we play against. The game has grown around the world, and the world includes the Confederation of North, Central American and Caribbean Association Football, the federation in which the United States plays. CONCACAF today is a competitive region. Six qualifying teams, forming what is known as the Hex, have a playoff from which three go on to the World Cup. For 2018 the six were Mexico, Costa Rica, Panama, Honduras, Trinidad and Tobago, and the United States. Players on many of these teams have gained experience in leagues outside their countries and bring that experience back to their national teams. Additionally, each country has experienced coaching staffs. The competition is keen and very real, and if you're not right in your planning and your actions, you can be left out of a World Cup, as we discovered.

Then there's the youth question. We need a fundamental shift in how US Soccer and Major League Soccer work together, with a priority on developing young American talent. How many times did you hear in this World Cup qualifying cycle that the pool of players we had available to us was the best it's ever been and we had a fine group of young players coming up? That was an exaggeration at best. How many young players in MLS are ready to play in senior international competition? I would argue very few. And that has to change—soon.

We need some fresh ideas. We can modify some playing rules and make adjustments in how we operate clubs and leagues at our various professional levels so as to accelerate the development of our younger players. Doing this will incentivize our young elite players to stay in our country. In return, the national team programs and our professional leagues will benefit. Every decision that is made must start with a disciplined look at what's best for the teams' chances of moving forward. Everyone has to be on the same page so that business choices take a back seat to competitive choices.

There is something about living through bad times that gives you perspective. I was amazed at how many people called or texted or e-mailed after the loss in Trinidad to tell me to take the long view and think about all we've accomplished over the years. Landon Donovan, for example, texted me in Trinidad, "Really sorry Bruce. You should be proud of all you've done for the team and this country." Former Cosmos great Shep Messing, who coached me years ago, offered this perspective: "Bruce has achieved iconic status as the greatest coach in the history of American soccer. . . . Contrary to the opinion of those who believe that the US national team's failure to qualify for Russia will tarnish Bruce's legacy, I believe that how he handled it only enhances it. Julius Irving said, 'Win with humility and lose with grace.' Bruce epitomized that with his statement after stepping down after the team's defeat."

I guess there's a reason why only seven countries in the world, the United States included, qualified for every World Cup from 1990 to 2014. International soccer is a serious business, and we've had the luxury of being complacent. I'm convinced that we're not that far away from where we need to be. The changes we need to make won't be easy, but they also won't be *that* difficult, and with those changes, we will grow stronger and continue to develop an American way of soccer that is self-confident, playing to our strengths. My seventieth birthday is not that far away. I don't know how much time I have left, but I'm optimistic I'll live to see the day when the US side are World Cup champions.

Part I

The Making of a Coach

Coaching

I can point to the exact moment, pretty much, when it dawned on me how huge an impact a talented coach can have on the outcome of a given game. I wouldn't say I was exactly cocky as a high school lacrosse player growing up on Long Island, but I knew I was good. In fact, when I looked around at the field and watched my teammates and guys on teams we faced, it usually seemed pretty clear that none of them had an edge on me. I remember one time during my junior year, we were playing one of our rivals, Elmont Memorial High School, just a few miles away, which was wedged between Franklin Square, where I grew up, and the borough of Queens, New York.

I'll never forget it. I was playing pretty well, and none of these guys on the Elmont team were all that good as individuals, but all of a sudden it's the end of the game and they've smoked us by some crazy score, 15–2 or something. It might have been the first time as an athlete that I stood out there on the field of play and consciously broke down how these players were being influenced. The Elmont guys were all disciplined, they were all fundamentally sound, and they were all selfless, team-oriented guys. Oh, and they kept looking over to their bench, at their coach, who was an enthusiastic guy, always talking to them, slapping a hand on their shoulder, trading a joke with them, talking to them in a calm, direct way about what they needed to be doing out there and how they needed to be thinking about the game. Clearly they were all on the same page, and clearly that coach had won these kids' respect.

His name was Richie Moran. He was another Long Island kid, who had starred in lacrosse at Sewanhaka High School in Floral Park, another community near ours. His high school team never lost in the four years he was playing there in the early 1950s, and then he moved on to the University of Maryland team that won the 1959 national championship. He came back to Long Island to coach Manhasset High School to the Long Island Championship every year from 1962 to 1964, finally moving on to Elmont Memorial, where I saw the impact he had on his players. I never had any great coaches in high school. They didn't seem to care about all the little things it took to influence the team. They showed up and went through the motions and went home and didn't give you or coaching a second thought. Richie Moran showed me the power of a coach with passion and vision and a commitment to all the little details of pushing for excellence.

I told myself: I'd love to play for this guy one day. And sure enough, he was hired to coach for Cornell University in Ithaca, New York, which was a top school, prestigious, Ivy League, all that. I knew I needed someone to take an interest, someone to believe I could amount to something. It wasn't like that in high school.

You know how you're supposed to sit down with your high school guidance counselor for a session on your future? My guidance counselor spent probably five minutes, tops, reviewing my file, and hardly looked at me when I came into her office. But, going by that deep understanding of what I was about, she decided the best I could do was leave Long Island and go to junior college in Hutchinson, Kansas, or maybe one of the New York state schools up in Fredonia. I sat there, trying to make sense of what she was saying to me, and looked at this lady and it hit me: *She thinks I'm a real fucking loser!* I left her office shaking my head, vowing to prove her wrong. Hey, maybe I wasn't the smartest guy around or the most talented or the most polished. I knew I hadn't applied myself, and I knew I had some rough edges, but I told myself: *I'm going to do more in my life than what this lady thinks.*

I grew up the son of a butcher. My dad, Vincent Arena, was a hardworking Italian man, not at all formally educated. His father died when my dad was in elementary school, and this forced my dad to leave school in order to work and provide for his family. That was the way things worked in those days. That was our world. Family was your first and last reference point. I had two older brothers when my mother became pregnant again. That had my parents worried, because having one more mouth to feed was going to put a real strain on the family finances. My mother went into labor and gave birth to Barbara, my sister—and then, three minutes later, there I was, not exactly a welcome surprise! My mother had no idea she was going to have twins. She couldn't stop crying when she saw me.

My mother was completely devoted to her family; she dedicated her life to us. Back then, women did not have careers in a formal sense. Their jobs were family. If my mother had been born at a later time, I imagine she would have had a successful career in business, law, politics, or whatever she might have chosen to do. She was an amazing woman—hardworking, bright, articulate, and demanding.

I was eight when my mother had her first surgery for breast cancer. She had two mastectomies and went back to her job driving a school bus. My twin sister, Barbara, was also hit by breast cancer, like many of my aunts and cousins on that side of the family, and died at thirty-seven. She'd been married only a year before, was really just starting her life, and it seemed that she'd put the cancer behind her after two mastectomies, but it came back and took her. That hit the whole family very hard. We lost my mother when she was sixty-nine, and of course that's always devastating, but at least we knew she'd lived a long and full life.

My brothers and I had to go through my mother's possessions to help get my father situated for life without her. We found out she'd managed to pay off our home, despite the fact that my parents provided for the family on the incomes of a butcher and a part-time school bus driver. All four children went on to college, and she'd also been able to sock away enough to have a decent savings account.

At her high school, in Brooklyn, you were required to learn a practical discipline, so besides getting straight As, she took up millinery and was an accomplished seamstress. She was so gifted, she made the wedding veils for all my cousins when they got married. Later in life she took up oil painting, and she wasn't dabbling. The paintings she did were beautiful. Today I proudly display four of her paintings in my home in Manhattan Beach, California. A special one is of my son, Kenny, and me at an early age in his life. Downstairs in the living room, we have one of Kenny in a cowboy hat, which always makes me smile. My mother was a special lady. I owe much to my parents for instilling important values that provided the foundation for everything I've done in life.

Sports was everything to us, growing up. In the summers I'd be out of the house early in the morning to play baseball all day long, trying to keep up with my brothers. My team was the Yankees and my player was Mickey Mantle. My father really didn't know much about sports, but he knew we loved the Yankees, so every year he would take us to two games. We'd sit in the right-center-field bleachers for one game, and for the other we got a box seat. How he ever did that on the income of a butcher, I'll never know, but those are some of the most unforgettable memories of my childhood. I can still remember that feeling of expectation and excitement walking into Yankee Stadium. My mother would pack sandwiches for us, and my father would have beers. He'd slip the cop at the front gate five bucks to look the other way, and we'd walk right in.

Those were the days of the twi-night doubleheader, so we were there all day and didn't miss a thing. I'll never forget being there in Yankee Stadium as a kid—old Yankee Stadium, I guess I've gotta say. Mantle and Roger Maris would be in right-center field, Frank Crosetti would be hitting fungoes from the third-base line, Clete Boyer would stand on third base with his glove right here, and these guys would throw ropes. Today no one in the outfield can throw. It drives me crazy. In those days, you weren't tagging up and getting in, with the arms those guys had. It was unbelievable.

My mother's father, Salvatore Schembre, had a deli in Brooklyn. Family lore has it that his was the first hero shop in the borough. I don't know for sure, but I could believe it. We would go there as a family and get these big heroes on Italian bread, piled high with meat. On the wall of the deli was a poster of the Italian World Cup team from 1950, the year before I was born. I didn't know anything about soccer as a kid, but that poster was always in the back of my mind. My grandfather had a DeSoto, and every Sunday we'd see him coming down the hill on Washington Street, before he turned onto Poppy Avenue. I remember how much we loved jumping onto the running board of his DeSoto as he parked in front of our house. He would step out of the car in a double-breasted suit, with a dark shirt, a paisley tie, his top hat and two-tone shoes, looking like a million bucks. He'd look around and call to my father.

"Vincente, get the ladder," he'd yell.

He wanted to trim trees. He'd be down to his T-shirt, pruning trees, until my mother called us all in to dinner. We loved his visits. He'd pull out a roll of cash and give each of us a five-dollar bill. That was a lot of money back then.

These were the years of the boom after World War II when suburbs were spreading all over the place. Franklin Square was near the planned community of Levittown, built just after the war, and looked similar. In ten years it all went from farmland to housing development after housing development. My school was right across the street from our house, first the elementary school, all the way through to high school, a stone's throw away.

The elementary school had a huge wall that became my best friend. I'd throw a ball against that wall for hour after hour after hour—baseball, lacrosse, soccer; that was how I learned and got better. I was done with baseball by the time I hit ninth grade. I'd thrown my arm out. I was a pitcher, and no one told me you're not supposed to throw the curve ball at that age, so I had so much pain, I used a heating pad on my arm every night just to be able to pitch. My brothers introduced me young to lacrosse, which was a popular sport on Long Island. They gave me a women's stick, which didn't really have a pocket, so practicing with that, my control was very good.

Lacrosse was my favorite sport all through high school. I was supposed to be a football player, like my older brothers. My brother Paul was the quarterback and star and then by his senior year, my brother Mike was in ninth grade, ready to take over as quarterback once Paul left. I was next in line after Mike, everyone figured. They made me quarterback of the freshman team, another Arena brother taking snaps, but it didn't work out well. I was maybe five foot three at the time, a hundred and ten pounds, and I had a left tackle who was six nine and more than three hundred pounds. It was like trying to throw over an oak tree. I'd drop back to pass and heave the ball with no idea where it was going. I couldn't see over this guy. It was so pathetic, I said no football for me.

I played lacrosse and wrestled, and because I was a wrestler,

I was always starving myself to cut weight. I wrestled at 103 pounds my freshman year, 112 my sophomore year, and 123 my junior year, and then I quit. Only then, when I quit, did something amazing happen: I started growing. All of those years of starving myself to cut weight stunted my growth. I wasn't growing because I didn't eat.

I had a friend who was on the soccer team, and at the end of junior year, he started working on me to join the team. I wasn't so sure. I didn't know the sport. Neither of my brothers played it. We never talked about it at home. But I figured I might as well give it a try. So I showed up for a practice, liked it well enough, and soon I was a starting midfielder. The first game of the season, our starting goalkeeper got in a fight and—boom—red card! He was out of the game and suspended for the rest of the season. The coach had no idea what to do. He called us into a huddle.

"Can anyone play in goal?" he asked.

No one said anything. The silence annoyed me.

"I guess I can," I said.

I started in goal after that. I took to it pretty quickly, since I had good hand-eye coordination after years of playing lacrosse and baseball. I was used to lacrosse, a sport that was developed by Iroquois Indians who lived in what's now New York before we got here, so it was always a regional sport. Soccer was the world sport. In my hometown there was a team called Hota, which played in the German-American League, and I ended up playing with their junior team. The senior team was largely composed of players from the New York Cosmos who played for Hota in their offseason. The club was literally a mile from my house, down the Hempstead Turnpike, at Plattdeutsche Park, where there was also a German restaurant. I showed up to watch a game and couldn't believe it. A crowd of several thousand turned out to watch the senior team play. Who were these people? I loved the energy and excitement. That got me into soccer.

Under Shep Messing's Wing

My brother Paul had a short stay at Nassau Community College, just six miles away from us, before transferring to Hofstra University. I figured if my brother could go to Nassau, I probably could, too. I knew they had a good lacrosse program, established in 1966 by Mike Candel. So when my high-school guidance counselor wrote me off as a loser and said basically I had limited options for college, I walked out of there thinking, *I'm going to Nassau, and then I'm transferring to Cornell to play for Richie Moran.* I made my mind up and that was just what I did.

I loved my two years at Nassau Community College. That was a special place. Instead of feeling that no one gave a damn, the way I always did back in high school, suddenly there was energy in the air and my classes actually interested me. It was a great time to be there. If you look up celebrity alums of Nassau Community College, you'll see some interesting people. The comedian Billy Crystal, a pretty good baseball player, I'm told, who even played a little soccer in high school, was at Nassau when I was, and his mother worked as the secretary in the athletic department.

His girlfriend at the time, now his wife, worked there too. Eddie Murphy, soon to make a name for himself on *Saturday Night Live*, was briefly a student at Nassau later on. Future actor Steve Buscemi lasted a semester before dropping out to work as a dishwasher, gas-station attendant, and fireman.

I found myself taking to studying for the first time in my life. I did well. It was a total switch from high school in every way possible. I was all-American in both soccer and lacrosse, and in my years there, 1970 and 1971, we won the first two National Junior College Athletic Association Lacrosse Tournaments. I even won a student-athlete award, if you can believe it. I wanted to walk back into my old high school and hand it to that guidance counselor, but I had better things to do with my time.

That was the beginning of my amazing run of good luck when it came to falling under the influence of great coaches. I'd taken up soccer late in high school and had very little actual idea of what I was doing as a goalkeeper. The best goalie in the country at the time was a guy named Shep Messing, who was born in the Bronx and went to high school at Wheatley in Old Westbury on the north shore of Long Island. Shep went to New York University for two years, earning all-American honors in 1968, but absolutely hated it. He bombed in the classroom and had a terrible relationship with his coach. He was so fed up, he dropped out and didn't think he even wanted to play soccer anymore.

As it happened, his former high school coach, Bill Stevenson, a great man, was my coach at Nassau. Bill was a good soccer coach and an even better person. He was wonderful to be around. We went out there every day with a smile because of him and loved training and playing games. Shep loved him even more than I did. Bill was the coach who had Shep for four years in high school and molded him into an athlete.

"Almost every professional athlete I've talked to remembers his coach, the one man, early on, who is still The Coach long after trades and quirky management decisions have placed him under a dozen grizzled authoritarians," Shep wrote in his 1978 book *The Education of an American Soccer Player.* "Stevenson was The Coach for me, and probably the reason I played soccer rather than football. He was a character right out of Clair Bee, the perfect combination of disciplinarian and nice guy. His techniques were textbook, and his coaching ideals were the traditional litany."

> Play your best, boys.
> Play clean.
> Don't talk to the referee.
> Damn well don't argue with the referee.
> Always pick up a fallen opponent on the field.
> Never scratch your vital parts on the field.
> Be stoic.
> Be sportsmanlike.

"And when the athletic director was not within hearing," Shep added, "he'd whisper these forbidden instructions: *Have fun.*"

Shep started taking classes at Nassau in 1969, coaching and working out with the team, though he was ineligible to play. Shep's mother was teaching at Nassau then as well. Instead of struggling in his classes, the way he had at NYU, Shep got straight As, and he helped Bill out as an assistant coach, working with the goalkeepers.

"You have a great athlete in goal," Bill told Shep. "He's a newcomer and he's a lacrosse player."

I learned more in one hour with Shep than anyone had taught me up to then, plus he was a great guy, with his wild outfits and boa constrictor. Apparently at some point he even did some modeling, which meant they gave him the crazy clothes they'd use for a shoot, so he was liable to wear a three-piece velvet suit or a silk scarf with a silver-knobbed walking stick or a Borsa-lino hat.

Shep was smart and was terrific at teaching the art of goal-keeping. I'd hit the jackpot. Shep molded me into a goalkeeper, starting from scratch, basically, since when I came to him, I was a raw athlete with no idea of the finer points of the position. I was like a sponge, soaking up whatever he had to offer. He influenced me in a huge way, teaching me how to train and the nuances of playing in the goal. He taught me how to dive. He showed me how to cut down angles and how to come out on the fast break, stomach to the ball, always stomach to the ball. You wanted to keep your stomach to the ball so you could get a piece of the ball on either side if the attacker tried to go by you. I could not have had a better goalkeeping mentor. Nassau was the perfect setting for me at the time.

Mike Candel, my lacrosse coach, was an extraordinary person. He was also the basketball coach at Nassau and—this is pretty amazing—went on to a long career as a sportswriter for different papers, including the Long Island paper *Newsday*, one of the best papers in the country at the time. Mike covered high school and college sports for *Newsday* from 1976 until he retired in 2002, and in 2017 he was inducted into the Nassau County Sports High School Athletics Hall of Fame. "Mike Candel could type fast, write fast and think fast, which helped him add sports writing to his resume that also included coaching and teaching at Nassau Community College," *Newsday* wrote in announcing his 2017 induction.

I learned so much from Mike. He not only taught me about lacrosse, but also he took me under his wing. He would go scout other teams we were about to play and bring me along to get my opinion. "He had a great eye," Mike told *New York Times* columnist George Vecsey in 2002. "When we played other teams, he had a talent for seeing what could be. He's always had this. . . .

Bruce was a lacrosse player who also played soccer. Don't get me wrong, he was a very good college [soccer] goalie, but he was an all-American midfielder in lacrosse. He was a tireless player, a joy to coach. He was one of those kids who would do what you told him. But in a million years, I would never have imagined him to be the national soccer coach!"

"Animal House" at Cornell

The lacrosse coach at Cornell University in the 1970s was Richie Moran, whose work back at Elmont High School on Long Island I'd admired so much. In 1969 he'd taken over from Ned Harkness, also a national-championship-winning hockey coach at Cornell, and in 1971 Richie won his first national championship for Cornell. I arrived the next year, and Richie took care of me. He found a place for me to stay, which was the SAE fraternity. I hadn't gone through rush or anything like that. I didn't pledge or go through any initiation. I just moved in to live with another Nassau transfer and ended up becoming one of the guys over time. It was great. Those guys are still my friends to this day.

It was like *Animal House*. Fraternities were huge at Cornell. You had all of these mansions that were fraternities. SAE had a beautiful Tudor-style house on McGraw Place built in 1914. That was where I lived my junior year. I loved being in Ithaca. It was just such a wild environment, so much going on, so many different students from all over, including international students, making for a very diverse, colorful mix of people coming together. I really enjoyed those two years, being around a lot of really bright people, including many of my teammates on the lacrosse team.

I went to Cornell to play lacrosse. At the beginning I wasn't even playing soccer. And if two of their goalkeepers had not hurt themselves, putting the team in a tough spot, I might never have played soccer at Cornell—or anywhere else. The injuries forced them to get creative, and Dan Wood, the coach, sought me out and asked if I would come play for him. Who was I to turn the man down? I came out and practiced for a week and then played in the NCAA Division I tournament.

My senior year, we beat Army 3–1 in the first round of the NCAA playoffs and Long Island University in the second, 3–2. The next morning's *New York Times* had a big picture of me fully stretched out to bat away a corner kick. Next up was a third-round showdown with our fellow Ivy League school, Harvard, where Shep Messing had played. We were considered underdogs to a team that was ranked number one in the country that year, but Victor Huerta, who set a Cornell record for points that year, used his speed and skill to score twice. The *New York Times* article, written by Alex Yannis, started with the words "Cornell upset Harvard" and continued: "Cornell's victory was preserved by Bruce Arena, the goalie, who thwarted Harvard's attack time and again."

That win over Harvard landed us in the Final Four, a first for Cornell, and we had to take on a tough UCLA team that included Sigi Schmid. The Bruins scored only one goal against me, but it was enough for a 1–0 win to send them to the final, where they lost to Saint Louis, a perennial soccer powerhouse. I ended up being named Most Valuable Defensive Player of the tournament and earning a spot on the all-Ivy team.

Dan Wood, the soccer coach, was some kind of genius. Seriously. He was a Phi Beta Kappa sociology major at Tufts and went on to earn a PhD in education at Cornell. He was also a great athlete, lettering in soccer, baseball, basketball, and tennis at Lehigh University before transferring to Tufts, and he was such a good golfer, he later joined the PGA Senior Tour and tied for seventh place at the 1998 US Senior Open at Riviera Country Club in Southern California. Dan's style as coach was different from Richie Moran's and that of other coaches I'd had. He relied above all on his intellect. He was so focused on soccer and the soccer team, it was as if he had blinders on. He and I are friends to this day.

The biggest influence on me, though, was Richie Moran. Lacrosse was my passion then, and I loved the way Richie ran our team. He embodied all the qualities of a leader; he was enthusiastic and upbeat, and he earned respect and influence, but above all he found a way to connect. I learned a lot watching Richie. He always saw you first as a person and second as an athlete. He followed your academic progress. He made sure you were a good person. My mother loved him. One thing I noticed, and never forgot, was the way he made a point of being the same with everyone. He had players on our team that weren't that good; they were at best peripheral to our success, but he made them feel every bit as important as every other player. I thought that was great, and I've tried to emulate that approach ever since.

Richie later talked to the *New York Times* about how he thought even back then I might have a future as a coach, based on what I'd say during the huddles we'd have during a game. "Bruce would come up with strategies," he told George Vecsey. "He would notice if we were overplaying somebody too much. He was always thinking a quarter or a half ahead."

Cornell prepared me to be a coach in so many different ways, from forcing me to connect with people from all sorts of different backgrounds and perspectives to opening up a world of learning that was so far beyond my miserable high school, I couldn't even believe it. Cornell attracted great minds like the Russian novelist

Vladimir Nabokov, author of *Lolita*, who lectured at Cornell a few years before I arrived. There was something in the air, really, an excitement about learning, an open-mindedness, almost a thirst for new knowledge and perspective. I hadn't been raised to see myself as a serious student. Our parents never asked us, "Did you do your homework?" In those days you didn't have that. There was no push. My older brothers, besides being star athletes, were also pretty sharp academically, so my parents just assumed I would be, too. High school never clicked for me. Nassau, and then especially Cornell, did.

I ended up majoring in agricultural economics and business management. I'd focused on business administration at Nassau, but at Cornell they didn't offer that as a major. So I went through the School of Agriculture, which did offer business classes, and that worked out, except that I had to earn a Bachelor of Science degree, rather than a Bachelor of Arts, and some of those required science courses were a nightmare. Chemistry was the worst. I had a professor who had won the Nobel Prize. I remember the first day of his class, my lacrosse buddy Jay Gallagher and I were sitting there, listening to him explain what was going to be required of us if we wanted to pass this class. Jay and I just looked at each other: *We are absolutely screwed in this class! We've got no shot.*

Then the professor added, "The tests are going to be multiple choice."

Like an idiot, I thought that was good for me. I was thinking, *Jeez, maybe I've got a chance.*

Wrong! For an exam on Civil War history or *Hamlet*, multiple choice is good. You can usually guess. With chemistry it was a disaster. You had no idea. None at all.

That class almost sunk me. I remember going to see the TA and saying, *I'll do whatever I have to do to pass this class.* I just wanted to pass chemistry so I could graduate, and I busted my ass trying to learn all this chemistry stuff that made no sense to me. I guess I learned just enough. Somehow I passed. It was insane. I couldn't stand chemistry, and I had to get through two semesters of it. Maybe college is really all about giving you an opportunity to learn to deal with doing things you hate and not losing all effectiveness.

My favorite class, without a doubt, was wine tasting, which was very popular, as you can imagine, with a couple hundred people jammed into an auditorium. It was taught by a Dutchman named Vans Christian, who tipped the scales at three hundred, easy. He was a character.

"You are going to graduate from Cornell," he told everyone in the auditorium during his opening lecture, even my fraternity brothers and me. "You are going to be in the world out there. You should be able to order a bottle of wine."

Fair point. He taught us all this practical stuff, like the ten things you should check on a wine label. Don't ask me to remember all ten! The grape variety or varieties, of course, the importer, the alcohol content, the year—I forget the rest. The class was on Wednesday afternoons from 2:30 to 4:30, but lacrosse practice started at 4:00, so I'd be there drinking for two hours and then head over to practice and play with a smile on my face, half bombed. It really was an education. The opening class was beers. A week later we focused on liqueurs. One week we tasted German wine, then French wine, then California wine. It wasn't like I felt a lot of pressure. The professor told us at the beginning, the class would be graded satisfactory/unsatisfactory; we just had to pass three quizzes, and there would be a paper due at the end of the semester, which we could write as a group. Well, I was there with a fraternity brother and a girl we knew, and she told us, "I'll write the paper. And by the way, I don't drink, so you can both have more of the wine." My fraternity brother and I silently agreed: *This girl's great!*

I first met my wife at a class at Cornell—Marriage, Family and Kinship. I couldn't help but notice this pretty coed sitting in my row, and I found out her name was Phyllis. In the class, we had the choice of keeping a journal or taking the final, and that to me was no choice. I wasn't about to keep a journal. Can you picture that? Me sitting down with a pen and a little book and writing about how I felt about my coaches or teammates? I also found it hard to show up at those lectures. Let's say it wasn't always riveting for me. Suddenly the final was coming up soon and I realized I had no notes to study and basically no shot at passing the class unless I got some help. I remembered sitting at an early lecture and one of my fraternity brothers knew Phyllis, who sat near us in class that day, and she looked like someone who would take good notes. I called her and asked if I could look at her notes. She agreed, and two years later we began dating. In July 2018, we will be celebrating our forty-second anniversary.

I remember studying all night with Phyllis's meticulous notes and going in there for the exam. I'm not going to say it was a cakewalk, but it was pretty much a classic Cornell test—write what you know in the blue book, have some connection to the contents of the course, and you knew you would be fine. Cornell was a great education, always challenging, usually fun, and in the end it left me always wanting to ask more questions, to understand better. Ithaca gave me a real education, not just a book education. That's how I function in life. Cornell wasn't going to make me book smart. That wasn't in the cards. But it did help me to know what I know. It taught me common sense.

The wine course came in handy, too. As a coach, it's amazing how often people give me bottles of wine as a gift. I'm not complaining. I enjoy a bottle. And I'm glad I learned a little something, but really, I'm not sure it matters. I have this theory, and it's the same thing with sushi: I really believe no one knows the difference between good sushi and bad sushi, and I also believe no one necessarily knows the difference between a really good wine and a lesser bottle. I've had five-hundred-dollar bottles of wine that were good and I've had forty-dollar bottles of wine that were real good. I always ask, "Do you like it?" If yes, then it's good wine. I don't get really hung up on all that stuff.

The National Team

had no clue where I was headed when I graduated from Cornell. I saw myself as a lacrosse player more than a soccer player, and I didn't feel like giving up either one just yet, but I was also angling for any work I could get that would help me develop as a coach. Richie Moran let me coach the freshman lacrosse team at Cornell, but that wasn't going to keep me in beer and pizza. I needed to make a little more money.

I had no plan, but I did have a purpose, and in those years I learned some valuable lessons in the art of improvisation, which is what soccer is all about. Be unorthodox and get creative and learn. Can you picture, for example, Mr. Arena, typing instructor? Or math teacher? Me neither. But that's what I was for a time. I remember I was sitting around with all my buddies from Cornell, and someone saw a classified ad from the city school district saying they needed help in the business education department. So I put on some decent clothes, combed my hair, and went to see the chairman of the business education department at the senior high school.

"We've had a lot of problems," he told me. "We've lost a few teachers. We need some help with our ninth-grade general business class and also the typing class."

I thought he was just telling me about his problems. I tried to look supportive and nodded a lot. I couldn't imagine that he wanted to put me in front of a classroom.

"Come back tomorrow," he said.

I showed up the next morning, and he brought me into this classroom with about twenty ninth-graders, all but one of them girls.

"I'd like to introduce you to your new teacher, Mr. Arena," he said, then turned around and walked right out the door.

You gotta be kidding! I was already thinking of the fun I'd have that night telling the guys about this. "You aren't going to believe it!" I'd tell them. "I'm a teacher now!" Which was just what I did that night. But first I had twenty students all staring at me, expecting me to say or do something. I bought some time by having them all introduce themselves and talk about what they'd learned so far, and basically killed time until I could go home and try to come up with some sort of plan for the next day. My next class there was typing, so I had to learn asdf and jkl and all that. It was like a master class in staying cool and collected even when you have no business staying cool and collected.

In February 1973, right in the middle of my senior year at Cornell, I'd been drafted by the New York Cosmos of the North American Soccer League with their fifth and final pick. I trained with them a little bit, despite the fact that at the time I was fully immersed in my season as captain of the Cornell lacrosse team. Shep Messing was the Cosmos' goalkeeper, and it was great to see him and work out together again. They offered me a contract, but I was never really tempted. I wasn't about to leave Cornell. I loved everything about my time in Ithaca. I was captain of the lacrosse team and an all-American, I'd made a splash as a goalkeeper in soccer. I had no interest in giving that up to earn two hundred bucks a game as a backup goalkeeper in the NASL. It was the right call for me, and only later on looking back did I ask myself how my life might have gone if I'd signed that contract. In June 1975, the Cosmos rocked the soccer world by signing the most visible player on the globe, Pelé. The great Brazilian was thirty-four by then, and he was a showman. "You can say now to the world that soccer has finally arrived in the United States," he said at the 21 Club in Manhattan during his welcome press conference.

The Cosmos' coach, Gordon Bradley, was also coaching the US national team. He saw potential in me, and later in 1973, after I'd graduated, he invited me to come play with the US national team abroad. I was going to join the team in Port-au-Prince for a game in early November against Haiti, but I couldn't make it. I think I'd already committed to leading Study Hall or something at the junior high. So instead I was on my way to Italy and Israel.

I was thrilled to be traveling out of the country. We played in Italy against their under-twenty-one team, and as a proud Italian American, I couldn't believe my luck in finally getting to see the country of my grandparents. To this day I swear that not everyone on our team was a US citizen, but we played even with Italy. I didn't play in that game; Bob Rigby was the goalkeeper, but I'd get my shot in Israel.

First, though, we had to get to Israel, which was not easy. We went to Rome airport to board our Pan Am flight to Tel Aviv, only to find that our flight had been canceled. This was November 1973. On October 6, the Yom Kippur War had broken out, with Egypt and Syria launching surprise attacks on Israel. As we were trying to fly from Rome, the United States was about to announce a cease-fire between Egypt and Israel. They got the team together, there in Rome airport, and asked us if we all still wanted to go to Israel or if anyone thought it was too dangerous. We were unanimous: "Let's go." We spent hours in the airport before they finally got us onto El Al, the Israeli national airline, which was the only airline still flying to Israel during the war. Back then security at airports was usually nothing, but we all got a taste of the future that day: let's just say the Israelis were meticulous in searching all of us.

It was a goodwill visit more than anything. We visited hospitals to show our support for the Israeli people. I'll never forget visiting the Wailing Wall in Jerusalem, the kind of place with so much history, you're speechless standing there. Our team captain, Barry Barto, remembers going into a movie theater on that trip to catch a screening of a political thriller called *The Day of the Jackal*. "A soldier leaned his rifle up against the back of my chair and that rifle was there the whole time I sat there watching the movie," Barry recalls.

On November 13, we played a match against Israel in the Tel Aviv suburb of Jaffa, losing 3–1, Bob Rigby in goal again, the stands filled with Israeli soldiers with machine guns looking for something to shoot. Our forward Willy Roy said later he played a great game, since all he could think about was running nonstop to avoid being a sitting duck when the shooting started. Two days later we went to Beersheba for another game against Israel.

It was war, so of course shortages were rampant. No one left their houses. They were all hiding inside. It was late at night when we arrived at our hotel in Beersheba, down in the Negev Desert in southern Israel. There was no one there, and no food to eat— and we had no idea where to go to get food, or if that would have been a crazy thing to try. All we had was a plate of tomatoes and celery, something like that, and a couple bottles of Scotch. Our preparation for that game was sitting around an abandoned hotel lobby drinking Scotch. The next day Bob played the first half in goal, giving up two goals in quick succession early in the game, and I played the second half. I don't remember much about the game, but that was my one cap. Coach Bradley, who was in his

early forties at the time, actually put himself into that game because the team was so depleted by injuries, and earned his only
cap as a player-manager. It's easy to forget that sports can matter
in a way beyond the playing field, but that trip to Israel showed
you the power a game can have.

The mayor of Beersheba hosted us for a lunch, thanking us all
for coming and talking about soccer as the international game
that brought people together. At one point he raised his glass,
citing an old saying, "If you drink the water, you will return."
Some of the guys put their glasses down, but it was an amazing visit, the experience of a lifetime in so many ways. We were
the first country to visit and play Israel after the Yom Kippur
War. "Those two games with Israel did so much for the Israeli
people," Gordon recalled. "I firmly believe there's a world family
of soccer."

I was drafted first overall by the Syracuse Stingers of the National Lacrosse League, a short-lived professional league in the
1970s. This was not outdoor lacrosse, my sport in high school and
college, but box lacrosse, played indoors. The Stingers lasted only
one season, finishing 12-27-1 in 1974, and then getting bought
and relocated to Quebec. They were going to be coached by Richie
Moran, but that didn't work out, so I never joined them except
to play some preseason exhibitions. Instead, I lived in Montreal
in 1975, playing for another team in the league, the Montreal
Quebecois. I was one of the few Americans playing in a league
full of crazy, rowdy Canadians, kind of like the Hanson brothers
in the Paul Newman movie *Slap Shot*. This was lacrosse with
hockey attitude: players were basically licensed to smack you with
a wooden stick wherever and whenever they liked. I had a blast
and finished the season with forty-five goals and forty-five assists.

It was a small league, with teams in Boston, Philadelphia, Maryland, Long Island, Quebec, and Montreal, so the travel wasn't real
heavy. We were one of the better teams and ended up going to

the championship game but losing to Quebec. I loved my time in Montreal, a picturesque city that felt more like Europe than North America. Our home games were at the old Montreal Forum, a cathedral of hockey, and even though I wasn't much of a hockey fan, I respected what the Montreal Canadiens had accomplished over the years. Their coach, Scotty Bowman, one of the greatest North American coaches ever in any sport, was just getting started but was well on his way to winning five Stanley Cup finals in the 1970s alone, an amazing feat. Scotty had superstars like Guy Lafleur and their goalie, Ken Dryden, a Cornell grad, but he seemed to talk to all of his players the same and keep them focused and alert. I made a mental note that when it was my turn to coach full-time, I'd try to do the same.

Dan Wood, who recruited me to play soccer at Cornell, landed a job in 1976 coaching in the old American Soccer League, a weaker rival to the North American Soccer League. Dan called me up and asked if I wanted to move out to Tacoma, Washington, to play goalkeeper for him. Of course I did! Phyllis and I moved out there, and it worked out well for me. When I first arrived, I was backing up a Brazilian goalkeeper who might have had some talent; it was hard to say, because this guy had the work ethic of Norm from the TV show *Cheers*. He got hurt, which made me the starter, and I had a lot of fun traveling around the West for games. People tend not to remember the American Soccer League of the 1970s, but there was a lot of excitement and fun. Bob Cousy, the Boston Celtics' Hall of Fame point guard, was the commissioner of the league, and they decided to use a red, white, and blue ball, like the red, white, and blue basketball Dr. J and others made famous in the American Basketball League, which was folded into the NBA in 1976.

The Tides played at Cheney Stadium, home also to the minor-league Tacoma Twins baseball team; it had a capacity of 6,500. I was in goal during the pregame ceremonies for the opening game

of the season, standing out there on the field, and they brought
in a helicopter to hover high over the field. Everybody loved that.
It jacked up the crowd. Then out of this helicopter comes flying
a red, white, and blue soccer ball. They misjudged the height,
obviously. It came from so high up, it pounded the grass like a
mortar shell, and then bounced so high, it flew right over me, the
goal, and the right-center-field fence behind me, and it was gone.
That was our only red, white, and blue ball. We had to go black
and white instead.

The level of play was actually pretty good. Mostly we played
the other teams in the Western Division: the Oakland Bucca-
neers; the Sacramento Spirits; the Los Angeles Skyhawks, who
played at a high school in the San Fernando Valley; and the Utah
Pioneers, who played in Salt Lake City. We made one trip to the
East Coast and played Cleveland, Rhode Island, and New York;
for me as a New York kid, it was a memorable homecoming. We
finished in second place in the West, losing in the semifinals to
the LA Skyhawks, who were the champions that year.

Phyllis and I had been living together for more than a year.
Somewhere along the way, without making too big a deal out of
it, we decided maybe we ought to get married and ended up having the ceremony in Tacoma on July 3, 1976, the day before the
United States' bicentennial celebration. It turned out that it really
didn't make sense for Phyllis's parents to fly out for the wedding.
Her father had worked as an engineer for the Grumman Aero-
space Corporation, which built the F4F Wildcat and F6F Hellcat
planes that helped us win World War II and later built the lunar
module that ended up on the moon during the Apollo Space Program. We carried on without them and went no frills all the way.
The ceremony was in my living room, presided over by the justice
of the peace, and we invited about thirty people, a lot of them my
Tacoma Tides teammates.

I remember, almost everyone was there, kind of milling around, and it was past the time we'd set for the ceremony, but my best man, Kenny Winzowski, hadn't showed up. Kenny and I went way back; he was the captain of the Montreal Quebecois, and we always had a blast together. Phyllis and I later named our son after him. The day before the wedding, Kenny had gotten friendly real quick with Phyllis's boss, and the two of them were driving around that afternoon. We later found out Kenny had driven her Porsche off the road, but we didn't know that at the time. It wasn't totaled or anything, but they didn't show up for quite a while. I gave Kenny a little time and then said, screw it! Mike Waldvogel, the assistant lacrosse coach at Cornell, was my first option off the bench. He stepped in and did just fine as my best man. We played records and danced, and a good time was had by all, but we had a game the next night, so Phyllis and I never had a honeymoon.

I was looking forward to another year in goal for Tacoma, but soon after the end of the season, the league folded. Fortunately, I had a backup plan. The vice president of the University of Puget Sound, a small liberal arts college on a beautiful campus in northern Tacoma, had called and made me an offer.

"Would you like to coach the soccer team?" he asked me. "We'll give you three free graduate courses."

I liked the sound of "free" and decided it was time to take some courses and work toward an MBA there. Pelé arrived from Brazil to play for the New York Cosmos that year, and there was a lot of talk of soccer *arriving* in the US. Seattle had a team in the NASL, the Sounders, that was doing well, and the Pacific Northwest seemed a fertile area for the growth of the sport. Even so, trying to build a college program from scratch at the University of Puget Sound was a challenge. I remember my assistant coach and me standing in the central quad area on campus and looking for anyone athletic-looking.

"Excuse me," we'd say. "Have you ever played soccer before?"

That was my first time coaching soccer, and to say I was learning on the job would be an understatement. I'd been lucky to watch a lot of great coaches in action and tried to borrow from them wherever I could, but it's different on the inside looking out. I'm not going to say I had some lightbulb go off in my head, like, *I've found my life calling!* I loved the challenge, but then, I'd loved the challenge of trying to teach typing to ninth-graders. Well, maybe "love" is a little strong, but I do always get up for a good challenge. Coaching a ragtag band of would-be soccer players was a lot more fun. I was feeling my way, but at least I understood the sport—or thought I did. I had a lot to learn. Good thing it was Division II.

I decided to try out for the Seattle Sounders, no matter how long the odds might have been. I knew right from the start that I wasn't going to make the team. I could just tell. But it was a learning experience that stayed with me. Why? It was a team dominated by English players and coaches, and I met some good guys, like Mike England and Steve Butler, but I also ran into some real assholes. They treated me like an absolute piece of shit, not because of anything I said or did, and not because I wasn't a good athlete. That experience left me with a bitter taste in my mouth.

I've had a bug up my ass for as long as I can remember about people from other countries looking down on anyone in soccer who comes from the United States. Back then, even the top college programs, like Howard and San Francisco, even Ivy League schools like Brown and Harvard, all relied heavily on foreign players. I decided back then that I was on a mission to show that Americans could play this game with the best of them—and that Americans could coach this game with the best of them as well. I didn't make the team in Seattle, in case that wasn't obvious. But I got something out of it.

Phyllis landed a job in Rochester, New York, and we decided to move back there. In making the decision to head back east, I was leaving more than Tacoma behind, the way I saw it. I was leaving behind the idea that I had any real future as a professional athlete, even though I knew I was good enough. I was probably the best American lacrosse player in Major League Lacrosse, looking forward to coming back the next year and making a decent income. But what do you know? The league folded. Then I went out to Tacoma, really enjoyed playing, and would have liked to keep it going, but after one season the team folded. It was too many starts and stops. I finally had to say: I'm not *doing* this anymore!

I got a call about going over to Hawaii to play for a new NASL team, which was going to play in Honolulu's fifty-thousand-seat Aloha Stadium for the 1977 season. It sounded nice, right? But I'd had enough. I could see just how it would unfold: we'd move all the way over to Hawaii, get set up over there, and then the same bullshit would happen, and we'd be stuck over in Hawaii. How was I going to make a living? Riding one of those bicycle taxi things around? Fat chance. I said, screw it! And sure enough, the team folded after one season, getting some of the worst attendance in the league.

When I left Tacoma, I'd decided I was not going to play professional sports anymore, but I did stay active with lacrosse for a while, playing some club lacrosse. I'd played on the 1974 US team that went to the world lacrosse championships in Melbourne, Australia, and won gold. Four years later we were in Manchester, England, of all places for the 1978 world championships and we looked unstoppable, beating Australia 22–17 and Canada 28–4, then just getting past England, 12–11. In the final against Canada, we gave up six unanswered goals early and fell behind but found a way to come back and force overtime. That was one exhausting match. We finally lost in overtime, 17–16. I think I scored three of the goals.

When we headed East so Phyllis could take her new job setting up weight-loss clinics, I figured I'd try taking some graduate classes at the Rochester Institute of Technology to keep working toward an MBA. I took a job working as a sociotherapist in a home for emotionally disturbed children. These kids were troubled, so you had to be delicate with them. My wife would laugh, hearing me say it, but working with those kids, I learned to be more tolerant and patient. I had my eyes opened about how lucky I was to have the family I had growing up, and the difference that made for me. These kids had no advantages. If you helped them, if you saw you were making any kind of a difference in their lives, you had the feeling that that really counted for something.

It didn't take me too long to figure out that I didn't want to wear a suit and work on Wall Street. I wasn't going to be a teacher. I wanted to be a coach. That was my passion, so we left Rochester and moved back to Ithaca, and my old coach, Richie Moran, gave me a position as junior varsity lacrosse coach at Cornell. I was chasing my dream again.

Back in Ithaca, I ended up getting a job as a high school truant officer, an interesting job in a lot of ways. In the mornings I'd go around to the schools, check attendance and find out who was missing. If there were issues with certain students, I might find out where they lived and go check up on them. That was another job that taught me something about keeping potentially tense situations from escalating. Make yourself clear, speak calmly, listen to what you hear in return, and expect good things. Generally that approach worked—and I did the job only a few weeks before I was back in the classroom teaching again. I even ended up teaching math for a while, which was a joke, of course. I briefly taught one of the sons of Carl Sagan, the astronomer. Me, teaching math to Carl Sagan's kid. Can you believe it?

The teaching I did here and there at that point in my life seemed like a lark at the time, but in the end it might have been as important to my future as any class I took at Cornell or Nassau

Community College. Those are things that you need to experience. It's an important background to have, because coaching is teaching. You deal with all kinds of different people, and you have to find common ground. I always ask myself the question about any player I coach, "How does he learn?" and that's something I started asking myself way back then in those classrooms. No two people are the same, and you have to have a sense for that.

To coach you have to be alert. You have to be open to improving your communication with each one of your players, always, even if it means trying something new. It always amazes me when someone gets an important coaching job based on past experience as a player. Being a great player is a good first step, but if you're ever really going to learn coaching, you have about a million other steps to take as well. You need training. You need experience. You need a lot of help in learning from others along the way and putting what you learn into practice. You hate to see coaches with not nearly enough preparation being thrown into the deep end, given the responsibility of running a team when they're not equipped to succeed. Then all the critics and pundits come out and start taking potshots.

UVA

Even now, more than forty years after I started coaching, I still can't believe my luck in getting to do what I love. If I meet someone new and they ask me how I make my living, sometimes I think about it and have to laugh.

"I've never really had a job," I tell them, which is true.

A job is something you do out of duty. A job is something you do because it's required of you. I've never gone down that road. All I've ever done is things that I wanted to do. I thought about a career in business and then thought, *No way. Not for me. I'm not about to go nuts sitting there in an office in a suit trying to fit in. I'd be bored out of my mind.*

I've been lucky enough to go from one fresh challenge to another, getting to work with great people and always finding a way to keep moving forward. I'm the first one to talk about hard work and attention to detail. I'm the first one to talk about trusting the people around you and going the extra mile—or sometimes the extra six thousand miles—to keep a relationship strong or to keep it from veering in a direction that might come back and bite you in the ass later.

Back in my early days of coaching, my friends kept telling me about job openings. Usually it was a stretch. Phyllis and I were living in Ithaca again in the spring of 1978, both working. Richie Moran was still the lacrosse coach at Cornell, and he had me back again that year, this time coaching JV lacrosse, not a full-time job but a lot of fun. Along with that I was still doing some teaching and mixing in a little bartending. We lived on Cayuga Lake, a great place to go for walks with our golden retriever, Josh, whom Phyllis got when he was a little puppy and brought to me in Montreal when I was playing professional lacrosse there. We were thinking we might buy that house on the lake and make a life there. You could do a lot worse.

I got a call from Dan Mackesey, who was a captain of the freshman lacrosse team I coached at Cornell a few years earlier. He was a law student at the University of Virginia by this time and had heard of a job opening.

"They're looking for, of all things, an assistant lacrosse coach who can also be the head soccer coach," he told me. "I thought of you right away."

How many schools even *had* programs in both soccer and lacrosse in 1978, let alone needed someone to coach both? I didn't think I had much of a chance. After all, my coaching résumé was thin. But I applied anyway, just to see what would happen. Would you believe it? They actually had me down there for an interview.

So I went down to Virginia and, I'm not going to lie, I was a total fish out of water. I was sure I had no chance at all. But the interview went pretty well. Actually, it went really well. Gene Corrigan, the athletic director, made clear that even though I'd be an assistant lacrosse coach and head soccer coach, lacrosse was their focus.

"Listen, just keep the guys on the soccer team happy," Gene told me, "but we want to win the national championship in lacrosse."

This was the South, not Mississippi or Alabama, but part of the

South. It was a big adjustment for us. I remember soon after we arrived saying to Phyllis, "We can stay a year and then leave." We were a long way from feeling comfortable. A guy in the athletic department started calling me Yankee, and the nickname stuck. I was the New Yorker. Everyone there hated the New York Yankees. That was in the Reggie Jackson era. He came out with a candy bar, the Reggie bar, and I bought a box of those and would throw them around when I came into the athletic department. It was a university with no diversity at the time. During my eighteen years there, it grew in diversity tremendously and was just a magnificent university and community.

I was coaching both soccer and lacrosse, and when I arrived, I discovered I'd inherited some other duties as well. I had somehow missed in my job interview the part about how I'd be expected to teach three PE courses. My first assignment was to teach tennis.

"But I don't even know how to play tennis!" I said to the head of the PE department.

"Figure it out," came the answer. "You'll be fine."

Gene Corrigan, the athletic director, was supposed to teach the tennis class with me. I showed up the first day of class, and Gene wasn't there. I was alone with fifty girls in their tennis clothes, me standing there with a clipboard trying to figure out something to say that wouldn't sound too stupid.

"Go ahead and play," I told the class. "We'll evaluate you based on your play."

Gene finally showed up, wearing a three-piece suit. He was the athletic director, after all, and had just come from a meeting with the president of the university. We got through the class somehow. Those first years at Virginia were all about learning on the job, but there were so many great people around—like Gene, who later moved on to Notre Dame—that you were always learning something.

If you asked me the best time I've ever had in my coaching career, I'd have to say it was at the University of Virginia. To this day, I'm in touch with most of the kids who played for me. You have an influence. In professional sports, it's just different. Players basically want to know: how much are you going to pay me, and how much are you going to play me? Everything else is secondary. I'm being blunt, but it's true. Working with some of the top professionals in the world has its upside, especially the quality of the soccer itself, but it's just not as enjoyable as coaching at the collegiate level. However, there are certainly limitations in college. You're not working with the best players in the sport who are constantly being lured into the professional ranks.

I started out slow in my first real stint as a soccer head coach. Gene Corrigan had made it clear that as far as the UVA athletic department was concerned, the job of coaching the ragtag men's soccer team was only half a step removed from the three PE classes I was teaching. Keep them happy and keep them out of trouble. That was the directive. Lacrosse was the priority; that was where Virginia wanted to be a national power, and I was happy to do what I could to help head coach Jim Adams, an icon of the sport.

Adams grew up in Baltimore and played lacrosse all four years at St. Paul's School, then moved on to Johns Hopkins University, where he helped the lacrosse team to three national championships. His coaching career took off in 1958. That was the year he took over at West Point, after the previous lacrosse coach died of a heart attack, and led Army to an undefeated record and national championship, the first of four he'd claim in nine years at Army. Virginia had beaten Johns Hopkins to claim its first NCAA championship in 1972, and the school wanted more.

Jim was different from any coach I was ever around. He'd made his name at Army, and he was conservative and disciplined in his approach. He was also a great family man and a very honest, upright man who inspired universal respect. He did an amazing job of having his teams prepared. You can learn from everyone, especially the greats, even if their approach is different than yours. I think to this day I have a little bit of Ace Adams in my coaching style—just a little, but it comes in handy now and then.

The Virginia soccer team when I took over in 1978 was kind of a joke. There might have been fraternity teams on campus that could have beaten us on a given day. The other teams in the Atlantic Coast Conference were built around scholarship athletes from around the world, like the Nigerians who made Clemson a national contender. One of the Nigerians would usually be the place-kicker on the Clemson football team as well. North Carolina and Maryland, and to a lesser extent, Duke and North Carolina State, also made the financial commitment to foster good programs. Then there was Virginia, which, when I arrived, had less than half of a scholarship, and to be honest I'm not sure how we got that. Actually, it was one three-hundred-dollar scholarship and one five-hundred-dollar scholarship, and neither of the two players on scholarship was going to help us win ACC games.

I'd brought in my first graduate assistant in the fall of 1979. Paul Milone was a New Jersey guy, an all-American at Princeton who played one season for the Pittsburgh Spirit of the Major Indoor Soccer League, then decided to go to business school at UVA. Having Paul around gave us a real shot in the arm. I still had much to learn, and Paul's enthusiasm and energy really helped me get my bearings.

My best hire at Virginia might have been Bob Bradley, another New Jersey guy who played his college soccer at Princeton. Bob and Paul Milone had been roommates at Princeton, and when Paul told me Bob would be interested in working with me at UVA, I was intrigued. Bob had an interesting background. He worked at Procter & Gamble after graduating from Princeton and decided to enroll in the graduate sports management program at Ohio

University. At Ohio, Bob was named head coach of the soccer team, a Division 1 program, at the age of twenty-two.

"I had to figure out where I could do an internship—that was part of the degree—but I still wanted to coach, and Paul Milone told me I should speak to Bruce," Bob Bradley remembers now. "So I drove from Athens, Ohio, to Charlottesville to meet Bruce. We hit it off. I had ideas on the game. Obviously, he had his ideas. We would challenge each other. In the spring, when Bruce would have responsibilities with lacrosse, I would handle soccer for him more."

We were together only two years at Virginia, but those were some of the best times of my life. In February 1981, Phyllis gave birth to our son Kenny, named for my buddy Kenny Winzowski, who was supposed to be my best man but didn't show up. Naturally as a coach and a former athlete, I was looking forward to the days when we could kick a soccer ball and throw a lacrosse ball. I took him out when he was six years old to play lacrosse; it was about 100 degrees in Charlottesville, and he hated it so much he never played again. His first babysitters were Bob Bradley and his girlfriend, Lindsay Sheehan, now his wife. For years our families were very close. Every summer we'd rent a beach house on the North Carolina coast, and the Bradleys would come for a week or so, along with the Sarachans and other friends. We'd have a blast and always be talking soccer. No surprise that my son and Dave Sarachan's son both ended up as coaches—and Bob's son Michael will be a coach after his playing days are over—count on it. And my son Kenny is now working with Bob as one of his assistants with the new MLS team in Los Angeles, LAFC.

Early on, when I was still coaching lacrosse and Bob was my assistant, I pulled him aside.

"You should stay here at Virginia because in a few years I'm going to be head lacrosse coach and you can be head soccer coach," I told him.

Good thing he got a job at Princeton and didn't hang around and wait. That would have been a long wait. Soccer soon became my total focus.

My education as a young coach took a huge step forward thanks to an accident of architecture: at the University of Virginia, I was moved into a new office in the lower level of University Hall in the early 1980s. To make room for my new office, they divided up the locker room for the visiting basketball teams, putting up framing and Sheetrock to wall me off. In the new configuration I could hear voices. Before games, at halftime, and afterward I could listen in on visiting coaches talking to their players: Dean Smith, Jim Valvano, Lefty Driesell, Mike Krzyzewski, Denny Crum, Bobby Cremins—I heard them all. Dean Smith was like a professor. Jim Valvano was comical, boisterous. Lefty Driesell was just about what you'd expect from Lefty Driesell. Krzyzewski was just plain sharp. I also had the opportunity to learn immensely from UVA's basketball, football, and lacrosse coaches, Terry Holland, George Welsh, and Jim Adams. All these coaches had their differing styles, but mostly they trusted the foundation they'd established over years of success and talking straight from the heart, asking questions like: *Who are we? What will we find out about ourselves with the way we play?*

For me, that was an incredible experience. It sounds funny, but probably the biggest challenge for a young coach is finding who you want to be. Each coach has to find his or her own voice. The voice has to come from within, but listening to great coaches—instantly identifiable with a few words—teaches you volumes about how to connect with athletes. You learn what to say, what not to say, and in general how to communicate. That helps silence the questions constantly swirling around in your mind as a young coach: *Am I giving the players the right information? Is the team properly prepared? Are the players confused? Is the team confident? Are we making the right adjustments at halftime? How do we talk after a loss or after a win?* I was getting the opportunity to hear from the very best and to see how their preparations worked or didn't work. This was one of the greatest experiences I've had in my life, and it deepened my everyday focus on becoming as good a coach as I could be.

I never heard a speech from John Wooden, who won an amazing seven straight NCAA championships for UCLA, but I loved this quote from him: "It's what you learn after you know it all that counts," he said. I also love this one from Mike Krzyzewski: "A common mistake among those who work in sport is spending a disproportional amount of time on X's and O's as compared to time spent learning about people."

Those were unbelievable years at UVA. I was surrounded by people with open minds, curious about everything, and we learned from each other and helped each other grow and develop. Back in my high school years on Long Island, no one believed in me, no one helped me along in a meaningful way. Most of my high school coaches were going through the motions. Most of my teachers were bored with their jobs and distracted. They had no time for a guy like me, whom they wrote off as going nowhere. I never forgot that and was always thankful when I could learn from other people the way I did at Virginia.

Being a young punk coach, I was hungry to build the program. I'll give our athletic director, Gene Corrigan, credit. He was honest. I pushed him to give us some real support, starting with real scholarships, and he didn't budge at all.

"If I gave you six scholarships, could you beat Clemson?" he asked me.

I thought about it.

"No," I said.

"Then why should I give you six scholarships?"

I argued for the importance of building a program, but I didn't have the experience to back up my words. I myself didn't have a detailed road map of what we needed to do to go from nowhere to national prominence, but I knew I was going to get there—or get somewhere, anyway.

A couple years after I was hired, Gene had a great opportunity and decided to move on. He was hired at the start of 1981 to succeed Edward "Moose" Krause as Notre Dame athletic director, and to replace him, Virginia hired Dick Schultz away from Cornell as its new AD. I'd never gotten to know Dick back at Cornell, but now we were working closely together. He sat me down right away to ask me how I saw the future of the soccer program.

"What do you think you can do?" he asked me.

"Well," I said, "if we do it right, I think one day we can have a nationally ranked program."

Dick was a good man. He did not laugh in my face, even though we were still the doormats of the conference that year. He decided to let me try and gave me the six scholarships I needed to start building a real program. We made immediate progress. Bob Bradley did a terrific job as my assistant. He was an invaluable help to me; we clicked immediately and were soon learning from each other and growing together as young coaches. We also enjoyed daily exchanges with a brash young assistant women's basketball coach by the name of Geno Auriemma, who would go on be the winningest coach in the history of NCAA sports.

We'd built Virginia into a top-ten soccer school by 1982, starting out by doing our best to acquire the best local talent, then looking to Olympic development programs and word of mouth to find the most promising kids in Virginia and the Washington DC area. By 1983, with Bob as my assistant, we made it to the NCAA semifinals, where we lost to Indiana, 3–1, before the Hoosiers edged Columbia 1–0 in overtime to take the national championship.

When Bob moved on to coach at Princeton in 1984, I needed to hire a new assistant. My old coach at Cornell, Dan Wood, told me about a player of his from Rochester named Dave Sarachan who might make a good assistant. Dave was Cornell's MVP his senior year, then played two seasons for the Rochester Lancers of the NASL and some indoor soccer as well. Dave was as raw as they come. Away from the field, he was a fish out of water. That was fairly typical in those days. He had an education and a good personality and spirit about him, and you knew he would be a success in the business. Like many soccer players moving into the world, he had a few things to learn about actually having a job.

I wasn't actually a full-time soccer coach until 1984, when UVA agreed to let me give up my lacrosse responsibilities. I loved lacrosse, but I knew it was a regional sport that was unlikely to break through nationally anytime soon. Soccer offered much better opportunities professionally and a greater challenge, as well. I was sure that it was moving toward a much higher national profile, even if there were going to be some bumps along the way. The North American Soccer League had generated such excitement in the 1970s, making me wish at times that I'd agreed to join the New York Cosmos as Shep Messing's backup in goal and maybe been teammates with Pelé and Franz Beckenbauer; by the early 1980s, however, it was struggling. A sluggish national economy, with double-digit unemployment for the first time in decades, didn't help. The league had also hurt itself by expanding too quickly and by focusing too much on foreign players, especially high-priced foreign players. Sound familiar? Every team wanted a Pelé back then. By 1984 the league went under, leading to a lot of commentary over what went wrong. My time trying out for the Seattle Sounders answered that one for me: I was sure the future of the sport lay in developing more homegrown talent. We'd appeal to more fans that way. We'd grow the sport that way.

That same year, 1984, the Summer Olympics in Los Angeles were a huge hit, and soccer turned out to be surprisingly popular. Peter Ueberroth had asked Alan Rothenberg to serve as commissioner of soccer for the Olympics, and he obviously did a great job. There were multiple crowds of more than a hundred thousand at the Rose Bowl for Olympic soccer games, and FIFA (Fédération Internationale de Football Association) was so impressed that the way was cleared for the United States to host the 1994 World Cup. "The success of soccer at the Olympics that year was probably the thing that led to where we are today," Rothenberg says now. "Up until that time, FIFA wouldn't consider bringing the World Cup to the United States because they were worried about empty stadiums. When they saw full stadiums, including big ones like the Rose Bowl in Pasadena and Stanford Stadium in Northern California, as well as smaller stadiums in the East, they decided it was safe to bring the World Cup to the United States."

As our program at Virginia gained momentum, I went back to see the athletic director. "Maybe we should try to build a soccer stadium," I told Dick.

"What do you think we could do if we built a stadium?" he asked.

"Win a national championship," I answered.

Dick was in. We started working on plans to get a stadium built. For years a local industrialist named Harry van Beek had been saying UVA needed to build a soccer stadium. Harry was born in the Dutch city of Eindhoven and lost much of his family late in World War II when the Germans bombed the city after US troops had liberated it, killing his parents and six brothers and sisters. He made a career with a German plastics company called Klöckner Pentaplast and was ultimately asked to move to the United States to start a branch here. He remained a huge soccer fan and kept urging the athletic department to do more for the sport.

"Put your money where your mouth is," Dick told him good-naturedly. "Build us a stadium!"

So Harry pitched his bosses back in Germany on the plan to help fund a soccer stadium in exchange for naming rights, and got them to agree. The result was $1.2 million, a lot of money in those days, which funded the first phase of construction on what would ultimately be a $3.4 million project that was completed in 1992 and put Virginia on the soccer map. Harry was a huge part of that. He was a wonderful man. I got to know him and his family very well and always looked forward to seeing him. He was one of those men who treated everyone the same—the same respect, the same courtesy, the same interest—no matter who you were. His vision helped provide a beautiful home for men's and women's soccer and men's and women's lacrosse for many years.

Our first major national recruit was George Gelnovatch, who joined us in 1983 after being first team All-American playing for Wall High School in Wall Township, New Jersey. George led his high school to three New Jersey state championships and was also chosen, along with another New Jersey high school player, Tab Ramos, to travel to Leningrad in the Soviet Union for the Granatkin Memorial international youth soccer tournament. George scored the winning goal in the youth team's 2–1 win over the Soviet side. With George our program continued to gain national recognition, and we were only a player or two short of being in range to compete for a national championship.

Back then we had Olympic development programs in each state to identify the top players in each age group, so you kept tabs on those kids as they worked their way up. Everything was new and developing back then, and people who loved soccer would do anything to get involved. That was the period when I first met Sunil Gulati, who used to work for the Region 1 Olympic development program. He was an administrative assistant at the time to Chuck Blazer, and also doubled as a water boy during the games, but he was also a graduate student in economics at Columbia University in New York. Sunil was very energetic and ambitious and put his ideas on building soccer in the US down on paper and circulated them.

In July 1987, when the US Soccer Federation lost its general secretary, Kurt Lamm, to a heart attack, Sunil was named his temporary replacement. He was all of twenty-seven years old at the time. Once we landed the 1994 World Cup, there was more and more to do, and Sunil's profile grew.

I was the state coach for the ODP in Virginia and then moved up to be a regional coach, which gave me a chance to work with the best young players and see for myself what I thought. I wasn't dumb. I decided to go after the best ones and landed many of them. Building a team is an art, though. The great players are the ones everyone sees as major talents. To be able to put together a team full of diverse talents that will add up to something, that takes a real eye—and I was beginning to develop that in those early years in Virginia.

Another important milestone in building UVA into a national soccer power was recruiting John Harkes. He grew up near Newark, New Jersey, ten miles due west of Manhattan in a community on the Passaic River called Kearny (pronounced CAR-nee) that is very proud of being Soccer Town USA, as it calls itself. The Clark Thread Company of Paisley, Scotland, opened a factory near Kearny in 1867, leading thousands of immigrants from Scotland and Ireland to settle in Kearny, bringing with them their love of soccer. The mills hired all the best soccer players arriving from across the Atlantic and every boy dreamed of growing up to be a star. Starting in 1883, Clark Thread Company fielded teams that competed in the American Football Association cups, winning in 1885, 1886, and 1887. Scottish pride and love of sport went hand in hand.

I visited John and his family in Kearny in 1985 and felt as if I'd flown over to Scotland. There were several Scottish butcher shops where you could find steak pies, chopped beef-and-onion turnovers, empire biscuits, and of course, Scottish bread. At the Piper's Cove, you could actually buy yourself a kilt. I decided I didn't need to go that far. John actually grew up right across the street from a local landmark, the Scots American Club, a shrine to football. The Club proudly recounts local history on its website: "Ever since [the 1880s] there's been a mystical and magical relationship between Kearny and soccer—generation after generation has fallen in love with the game, a thread as long as the 150-year-old town itself."

Jim Harkes emigrated from Scotland and settled in Kearny in the 1960s, playing for the Scots Club team and meeting his future wife at a Scots Club social event. Their son John grew up with soccer in his blood. "The ball connects everybody, right?" John says. "People would ask: 'Where's this Kearny? What's happening there? Is there some kind of magic there? Is there something in the water?'" Jim Harkes remembers. John played on the Thistle club team, along with Tab Ramos and Tony Meola, suiting up before games at the Scots Club, where he'd hear the old-timers talking football, and afterward if he was lucky, his dad would get him some potato chips and a soda and let him hang out in the St. Andrew's Room.

When I visited the place with Jim and John, they joked that it hadn't changed much over the years. We sat at the bar and talked football with all the regulars, ordered a pint or two, and on Sunday morning you could sit there and watch all the games from Europe via satellite, which back in those days was a rarity. Recruiting isn't really all that complicated. I took the same approach to those meetings that I do to all meetings: focus on a few main points you want to make, don't ever try to bullshit anyone, and just relax and be yourself; if that flies, great, and if not, so be it. I was very confident about the future of Virginia soccer, and that came through.

Sometimes you found talent the way everyone else did, by picking up the newspaper. A Texas kid named Jeff Agoos was chosen as a *Parade* magazine High School All-American two years running, so we figured he was worth a look. Goose, as we all ended up calling him, was born in Geneva, Switzerland, when his dad was working over there for Caterpilliar Construction Company, but he grew up in Texas. I flew out to Dallas to see him twice. Usually if you connect with the family, you have a good shot at working well with the kid, and I really liked the Agoos family. They were thoughtful, interesting people you could talk to about almost anything.

Having John Harkes on the team might have helped in our appeal to Tony Meola, another Kearney kid. John was the Missouri Athletic Club's soccer Player of the Year in 1987. Over the years, other waves of immigrants, most of them soccer-loving, added to the mix, including a lot of Italians, as I'd noticed on my earlier visits. Tony's father, Vincenzo, played for Avellino in the Italian second division before emigrating to the United States, and Tony grew up in Kearney with soccer all around and a father who knew the game inside out and could pass that love on to him. Tony was a great three-sport athlete, later drafted by the New York Yankees, and we recruited him to Virginia to play both baseball and soccer. He'd played some forward in high school, but for us he'd focus on being a great goalkeeper.

That was quite a year for him. Tony was the starting goalkeeper for the US team trying to qualify for the 1990 World Cup in Italy, something no American team had been able to do in forty years. Tony came through with shutouts of Guatemala, El Salvador, and Trinidad and Tobago in World Cup qualifiers, and for us he'd been outstanding. As Michael Janofsky wrote in the New York Times that November, "These are charmed times for Meola, a rugged 6-foot-1-inch, 205-pound sophomore who has unusually large hands for a goalie and a stunning quickness that gets him in position to take advantage of them."

That might have been the first year when I felt all season long that we had the talent to win it all. I had the players, and we'd built momentum with the program; the challenge was finding ways both to keep people loose and to keep them focused. Sometimes you sacrifice one for the other, pushing your guys when you know there's a risk they'll get tight, or on the other side, backing off to let them find themselves. The guys still talk about the golden jockstrap we came up with that year. As Lyle Yorks recalled to the soccer website FourFourTwo:

> *In 1989, the first day of practice preparing for the NCAAs, he comes in and he's got a jockstrap, and it's spray-painted gold. It's really stiff, and it's hanging on a hanger. It was decided whoever performs best in training each day, the next day this will be hanging in your locker. And they'd cut your picture out of the media guide and staple it to the jockstrap. Everyone was so desperate to get the golden jockstrap, so we're turning up to training a few minutes early. The banter was unbelievable, and [the winner] could be who grinded it out, who battled the hardest—it could have been anything. It really took a life form of its own. We competed, as he would say, like bastards. And when we're heading up to Rutgers for the final four, we all get on the team bus, and they spray-painted a briefcase and put chains all around it, all spray-painted. That's how we're transporting the golden jock all the way up. And we ended up winning our first national championship. That's typical Bruce. We all rallied behind a jockstrap, and it ended up contributing on some level to our first national championship.*

That was the year that came down to one crazy game the length of two games, though it felt like the guys were out there for about a year. We'd won 4–1 over Philadelphia Textile, then had to go to overtime to win 1–0 over South Carolina in the second round, when Kris Kelderman scored in the 112th minute of play. We followed that up with a 3–0 win over Rutgers, so we were confident going into the final against Santa Clara, coached by Steve Sampson.

One thing I always hate doing is micro-analyzing a game before it's happened, so I might have been a little flippant when asked by a *Sports Illustrated* reporter the night before the final if I was concerned about weather reports showing we'd be dealing with bitter cold. "We'd play for the national championship in a parking lot," I said.

The game started at 12:30 p.m. and at the time the temperature was 21 degrees with a wind-chill factor of 10 below zero. As *Sports Illustrated* wrote, "It was so cold, in fact, that Cavalier striker John Maessner joked that he was glad when he got kicked because it gave his legs a warm glow." Lyle Yorks took a corner on the left in the twenty-seventh minute, Richie Williams headed the ball, and Drew Fallon finished to give us a 1–0 lead. We liked our chances of making that lead hold up, especially with Tony Meola in net, and for nearly sixty minutes of soccer it did, but then with just six minutes left in the game, Santa Clara equalized, sending it to overtime. That frigid wind was miserable. We played two fifteen-minute full overtime periods with no scoring, then two fifteen-minute sudden-death overtimes. Still 1–1. I was proud of my guys, but beside myself that one lapse cost us our goal for the season.

"No, I don't feel like a champion right now," I said afterward. "I think penalty kicks after the sudden-death overtime is better."

Our last major recruit in my time at Virginia was Claudio Reyna, another product of New Jersey with a foreign-born father. Claudio's father played professionally in Argentina for Los Andes after rising through Independiente's youth program, then moved to New Jersey, where he married a Portuguese American. Claudio went to Saint Benedict's Preparatory School in Newark, where Tab Ramos had also starred, and the team went 65-0 over his three seasons playing there, leading *Parade* magazine to name

Claudio its high school Player of the Year not once but twice. He joined us in 1991.

Harkes (1987), Meola (1989), and Reyna (1992 and 1993) all won national player of the year awards, and I think many would agree with me that those three would have to be counted as among the finest players ever in the history of US college soccer. They all went on to make a mark on the US program, which we'll get to, and they all contributed to our amazing run at Virginia, winning the NCAA championships in 1991, 1992, 1993, and 1994. John Harkes was with us three years and left before we won a championship, Tony was with us two years and left before we won a championship outright. With Claudio we won three national championships in three years, and the amazing thing was, even without him we won the next year. The class of guys he came in with won four NCAA championships, something very few athletes in the history of college sports can match.

I'd set out to build a program. I accomplished that. Here's a stat I'm proud of: As of 2017, UVA had qualified for the annual College Cup thirty-four years in a row, dating back to 1981, my fourth year as coach; that's more than any other team ever. That has to do with bringing in good people. George Gelnovatch, one of our first major recruits at UVA, went on to play professional soccer for several years, then came back and worked with me at Virginia as an assistant and took over for me when I left, holding the job ever since. It has to do with aiming high and selling people on a vision of achieving at the highest level. And it also has to do with thinking longer-term and understanding that infrastructure really does matter, the way that Klöckner Stadium mattered for us. It opened in August 1992, and we won it all each of the next three years. Having a brand new, soccer-specific facility with a capacity of eight thousand was a huge lift to the program, great for recruiting, and great for the guys. Dick Shultz was long gone by then, but I'd shown him I was a man of my word: *If we build it, the championships will come.*

One reason I enjoyed those years so much was that it was the right thing at the right time for me. As a young coach looking to learn, I couldn't have done better than having so many bright, energetic coaches around for sharing ideas, sometimes arguing, sometimes getting into a friendly little rivalry, but always learning and gaining more perspective. We were always together. We were challenging each other, questioning each other, and being motivated every day to be good at what we did. It was really fun. Today you can't do any of this stuff anymore. You have an HR person. You've got rules and regulations, a lot of which are ridiculous.

Back then we could go out for beers with the kids, hang out and talk; no one was looking over your shoulder. You could never do that today, at least not in the same way. I'm not even sure that nowadays coaches would play in summer-league softball together with students, but that's what we did then, and we had a great time. Our first baseman was Ralph Sampson, the center on our basketball team, and that was pretty cool, throwing over to a guy who stood seven-four, with arms so long he could snag just about anything you tossed his way. All the coaches played on that softball team: Bob Bradley, Tom O'Brien, Mike Archer, Geno Auriemma, Dave Odom, and Craig Littlepage. Looking back, I'm struck by how many of those coaches I hung out with then went on to great achievements. Bob Bradley is arguably as successful as any soccer coach ever in this country. Tom O'Brien went on to be the head football coach at Boston College and North Carolina State, and Mike Archer coached in the NFL for many years. Geno Auriemma has led the University of Connecticut women's basketball team to eleven NCAA championships—eleven! Dave Odom went from assistant basketball coach to the head coach at Wake Forest. Craig Littlepage was the assistant basketball coach then and went on to be UVA athletic director. All these people did great things. You expected nothing less out of yourself if you were part of that group.

DC United

One thing the rise of Major League Soccer did was force the US Soccer Federation to stop being so closed-minded when it came to looking for talented head coaches. Up until MLS started playing its games, the federation made clear that if you were US born, you'd be discriminated against. That's not quite how they put it, but that was the gist. It was all part of an inferiority complex that was its own problem—and in many ways remains a problem to this day. Even while I was still at Virginia, I spoke out against what I saw as bias.

"It's a closed shop," I told Paul Kuharsky of the *New York Times* in June 1995. "The federation has a tendency that when you're good, they feel threatened. Unfortunately, a lot of the decision-makers have limited real soccer experience. They know the names, they know the faces, but not the game. And they're making the decisions and telling us we don't have the experience. In some ways, it is just comical."

No one could accuse me of kissing ass! Comments like that might have made it harder for the federation to give me real consideration as coach, but I spoke my mind and never regretted it.

Blunt talk has always been central to how I do my job. The way I've always seen it, you ought to respect people enough to tell it like it is. They deserve more than to have you beat around the bush or tell tall tales.

I loved my life in Virginia, and had no immediate plans to move on. I had to explore the options, though. I wasn't sure at first what to make of the new professional league being created, timed to make the most of the wave of enthusiasm generated by the 1994 World Cup hosted by the US. I knew that the MLS team planned for the Washington DC area was going to be a dynamo, and since I already lived in the area, I was a natural fit. I'd heard about the main organizer of the new franchise, Kevin Payne, who ran a sports marketing company in New York and was administrator for the US Soccer Federation. He put together the supporters' tour for the 1990 World Cup in Italy. Phyllis, Kenny, and I were there, and that was the first time I met Kevin, though we didn't get a chance to talk much. Even then I was struck by his great passion for the game.

An October 1994 *Washington Post* article on plans for the new league quoted Kevin, mentioning that he was executive vice president of Soccer USA Partners, which had been responsible for marketing the USSF since 1990 and which would oversee the new Washington franchise. "We are very bullish about the sport and what's going to happen in the next four, eight, twelve years," Kevin said. "We're looking very hard at the opportunity, and we feel there's a real market for the sport."

As things moved along and got more serious, Kevin sought me out. Our first real meeting occurred in January 1995 at the Marriott Wardman Park in Washington. This was during the annual convention of the National Soccer Coaches Association of America (recently renamed United Soccer Coaches), and Kevin and I sat down to get to know each other and talk some things out. It's funny. A lot of articles have been written about me, talking about how I speak my mind and never hold back. It's true I like straight talk, but that doesn't mean I can't shut up and listen. Sometimes I like to hear someone out and give myself time to think about where I stand. That's my recollection of that meeting with Kevin. I was enthusiastic about the general idea of taking over as coach of DC United because I'm a builder; I always like to build something from scratch and do it right. I saw it as a positive, introductory kind of meeting. For the record, Kevin remembers us coming to a firm understanding that I would be the first coach of DC United. Even in that scenario, I still had another season of college soccer, and that was my focus. Either way, I was a long way from making the transition.

The job that intrigued me the most was coaching the US Olympic team. Going back to my time trying out in Seattle, I had some major attitude about the way "US" and "soccer" were treated as if they didn't belong together. My success at Virginia positioned me to be a candidate to coach the Olympic team into the 1996 Summer Olympics, which would be in the United States. The soccer tournament featured mostly younger players, twenty-three and under; plus, each team could have three older players. The games would be played throughout the East Coast.

When the news broke in September 1995 that the previous Olympic coach, Timo Liekoski, had been let go, speculation kicked up that I might be named his replacement. *USA Today* called me and asked me if I was interested in the job, and I declined to comment, but I did say I was surprised to hear Timo had been fired. "This is news to me," I said. "Timo has done a lot for US soccer. He's a first-class representative of soccer."

Soon I was flying out to California for a meeting with Alan Rothenberg, the president of the US Soccer Federation, as well as Kevin Payne, Steve Sampson, the coach of the US national team then, and Sunil Gulati and Hank Steinbrecher of US Soccer. I didn't even have to leave the airport. We met right there in the

Admirals Club at LAX. We discussed how I'd handle the team if I was given the job of Olympics coach. I had a few ideas and a few demands.

It was a great meeting, and they asked if I wanted the job.

"I'd be interested in that," I said.

"And you can also coach DC United in Major League Soccer," Alan said.

I was focused more on the Olympic job at that point, but it was all a great opportunity, no question. My head was spinning when I walked out of there. They'd been very clear at the meeting that everything we discussed had to remain confidential. Everyone agreed: no leaks. That was fine with me. I was happy for some time to think. I had great respect for Alan, a brilliant guy who was a kind of Renaissance Man with a variety of interests. He was a lawyer at a big law firm in LA and played a big role on the FIFA executive committee. I caught a red-eye out of LAX that night to get back to Virginia in the morning.

I'll never forget getting off my flight at Dulles Airport and stopping by the newsstand to pick up the papers. I pulled out the *Washington Post* sports section and there on the front page was an article about me.

Virginia's Arena May Coach D.C., Olympic Soccer Teams

Steven Goff, one of the most respected soccer writers in the business, was reporting that I "likely will leave the school after this season to coach the Washington franchise in a new professional outdoor soccer league and become the 1996 US Olympic team coach, sources said."

Sources? Who were these sources? I thought we'd all agreed to keep the LAX meeting confidential.

The article noted that over eighteen seasons at Virginia, I'd compiled a 286-57-31 record and at the time we were number one in the nation, working on a twenty-three-game unbeaten streak, so it was good publicity about UVA, but it created problems for me.

Goff had reached out to the University of Virginia athletic director, Terry Holland, and through a spokesman, Terry had said, "I certainly hope his ultimate decision is to stay at Virginia. But I will support any decision he makes."

Terry was a man of his word, too. I hadn't slept much on my red eye back to DC from LAX, but as soon as I saw that article, I knew I needed to drive straight over to campus, which was exactly what I did. Terry was great. We talked it over, and he told me what he'd told Goff: he'd support me in whatever direction I took. I stuck with Virginia through the end of the season, hoping to make it five national championships in a row, but wrapped up my UVA time on another cold day with a "stunning" upset loss to Duke in the semifinals, as the *New York Times* put it. "In what amounted to the big shot on the block being upstaged by the kid around the corner, Virginia's bid for a fifth consecutive national championship in soccer came to an end today at the hands of a league rival," Alex Yannis wrote.

We fell behind by two goals early and scored two to get back into it, but gave up a third goal that ended our run. I was stoic, I guess you'd have to say, afterward. "Soccer's a funny game," I said. "Sometimes the ball doesn't bounce the right way, and it didn't for us. But we've won our fair share of championships."

Coaching at Virginia was the most enjoyable job I ever had. Working with young men and having an influence on their lives was a very special privilege, but it was also true that I was coaching a short season that could take my talent only so far. As a competitor, I couldn't say no to this great new opportunity, but once again I had a lot to learn. This was a whole new world.

As my assistants I hired Bob Bradley and Glenn "Mooch" Myernick, who had won the Hermann Trophy as collegiate player of the year back in 1976, playing for Hartwick College, and had eight years in the NASL. Mooch focused on the Olympic team and Bob shuttled back and forth between the two teams. Bob remembers:

It was exciting, for sure. Everybody waited for there to be another professional league. The first year was incredible. And in the early part of the year there was still, for us, a focus on the Olympic team, and at times I just tried to be the balance, so that if Bruce had to spend more time on that, I could focus on DC, and at times he was a little more focused with DC, Mooch was still with the Olympic team, but I would always be there to help Mooch, so I tried to make sure I could help in all ways. . . . Mooch and Bruce and I rented an apartment in Chula Vista. We called it the cave, because it was below ground and had no light. And there were times when all three of us were there, and then there were times when one or another would be out, and the others would hold the fort.

I'd ruffled some feathers over the years for having a vision and sticking with it, and not being one to mince words. I saw no reason to change my style now, especially given the challenging hand I'd been dealt. If some in the press wanted to make me out as some kind of rebel, that was fine with me. I always liked James Dean. Who didn't?

This was the headline that December on me in *Newsday,* my hometown paper on Long Island: "He's a Rebel with a Cause: Virginia's Arena to Bring His Own Style to '96 US Olympic Team."

The article, by John Jeansonne, was kind of funny.

Arena, forty-four, has made a career of assaulting the system. He built soccer into a money-making sport at the

University of Virginia, which, like every Division I college, preferred to market basketball and football. He created teams that went beyond sheer dominance—four straight NCAA titles—to critically acclaimed aesthetics, playing what is universally described as "attacking, attractive, sophisticated soccer." He sought out the best American players at a time when most coaches found it more productive to sign up foreigners. He called the US Soccer Federation a "good ol' boy network." The chin is up, the eyes look down the nose a little, and the smile is a bit crooked and on the wise-acre side. Is it possible that this man experienced a time when he was considered an outsider? "Yeah," he said. "Like maybe now."

I had few illusions about what I was walking into. I knew we were behind the eight ball. We had to double up, focusing on both DC United and the US Olympic team at once. We were building a team from scratch to compete in a league just being formed and at the same time trying to build a competitive Olympic team comprised largely of collegiate players. That was a tall order, to say the least. Fortunately, we got great cooperation from everyone involved. Since we were out in Southern California at the Olympic Training Center in Chula Vista, next to San Diego, bringing in the Olympians at the start of the year, we set it up so that all the DC United players flew out to California that March and we trained them out there as well.

Here's how compressed everything was: On Sunday, February 4, I picked up my first international win as a coach when A. J. Wood, a former Virginia player of mine, headed home the game-winner near the end of regulation to give us a 2–1 win over Norway in a friendly in Jacksonville, Florida, a tune-up match for our Olympic team. Two days later, I was huddling with Kevin Payne on the first day of the Major League Soccer draft, working to make sure we were able to land our first choice, Raúl Díaz Arce, starting forward on El Salvador's team, with our first-round pick. I also wanted to load up on former Virginia players, for I knew what I'd be getting and they were proven winners, so we drafted defender Erik Imler in the third round, midfielder Richie Williams in the fourth round, and another midfielder, Kris Kelderman, in the eighth round.

We felt that we had a strong nucleus of talent, because we'd already had four strong players assigned to us as part of setting up the franchise: Jeff Agoos and John Harkes, two more UVA guys, and Marco Etcheverry and Juan Berthy Suárez of Bolivia. We had a combine in California where we brought in players, looking to round out our roster, but the truth was, we really didn't have a very good sense of what we were doing or what we needed. My approach to coaching is based on working hard on all the details behind the scenes so that when it's time to play, you let your guys play, but on the preparation side there were too many question marks for me to have a clear vision. As I've said before, it's not about finding the most talent; it's about finding the right talent that fits together to form a larger whole. There's always guesswork involved in doing that, but in putting our first DC United team together, we were too often deep into guesswork. Looking back, I can say that our first draft really wasn't as good as we thought at the time.

Going into the season, we didn't know who we were as a team or what we had. Once again, as for so many big games in my career, we were in San Jose, California, playing before more than thirty thousand people at Spartan Stadium, home to San Jose State's football team, and by *football* I mean the kind with touchdowns and field goals. Our game against the new San Jose team in the MLS, which at the time was called the Clash but would be changed back to the Earthquakes, was the season opener and therefore the first game played in the history of the MLS. We played to a scoreless draw at halftime, and late in the game it was still 0–0. Alan Rothenberg and Sunil and the other founders of the league were sweating it out. Then in the final minutes, Eric Wynalda scored for San Jose and yanked off his shirt and slid to his knees. "It's the best feeling I had scoring a goal in my life," he said afterward.

We were outshot and outworked. We knew we had a lot of work to do, getting the guys in better shape, which had been hard with storms raging in the East. "They deserved to win," I said of San Jose afterward. "They had more of a fight in them." I was blunt about how I saw Marco Etcheverry's performance in his first game for us. "He and John Harkes didn't play particularly well."

We lost our first four games, including our home opener, and despite having been built up going into the season as one of the best teams in the league, we found ourselves dropping to 1-6. We kept making changes, kept tinkering, and finally things started to get better. I limited Marco's playing time because I wasn't happy with what I was seeing. That lit a fire under him, and he demanded more minutes. Good! That's what we wanted to see. Some passion.

You build a team by reaching out to every player as an individual and trusting that you'll have an idea of the right way to get that player on board. Sometimes it's as simple as making sure they're comfortable with where they're living. For example, in 1997 I recruited Ben Olsen out of the University of Virginia to play for DC United at the age of nineteen. I suggested he move in with Phyllis and Kenny and me. "Just stay with us," I said. "You'll save some money. You'll eat better this way. You won't be eating that fucking Taco Bell all the time."

Finally, on May 15 at home, we had a breakout game, with Steve Rammel scoring the first hat trick (three goals by one player in one game) in MLS history and leading us to a 5–2 rout of the

Columbus Crew. By July we really had it going; we kind of had the feeling by then that we were the best team in the league. I'll admit, my head was spinning at times, trying to keep up with all the details of coaching both DC United and the Olympic team at the same time.

"Marco will take all the corners," I said at a practice in July.

The players were confused. Marco Etcheverry played for DC United, and this was the US Olympic team.

"Marco?" at least one asked, before everyone figured out I meant Claudio Reyna and just got confused. A little confusion went with the territory. I'd flown nearly forty thousand miles in three months, shuttling back and forth between the two teams. I could never have kept on top of it all if not for the great work of Bob Bradley and Glenn Myernick. I delegated a lot to them, and they stepped up.

Two years earlier, when the United States hosted the 1994 World Cup, everyone was talking about soccer and there was a real wave of excitement. At the same time, you still had to deal with the yahoos who just didn't get it. I was shocked when I found out that NBC, the network that had paid for rights to the Olympic Games, wasn't going to televise *our* games. Pure boneheadedness on their part, the way I saw it—and still see it now. "Soccer is going to be the Olympic event with the largest attendance," I told the *New York Times*. "How can that not be newsworthy to NBC?"

Worse than clueless network executives were clueless newspaper types. Some guy named Norman Chad wrote a column—the headline was THE JOY OF TESH—about how much he liked the broadcaster John Tesh. Does anyone remember him? Chad was probably being ironic when he gushed about "the somewhat majestic" John Tesh, but even if his enthusiasm was supposed to be a joke, it tells you all you need to know about Chad. This same guy had this to say about soccer, the world's sport: "Bruce Arena is complaining that NBC is not showing his team's games. Yeah,

Bruce, for the same reason NBC is no longer showing *J.J. Starbuck*. How many times do we have to go through this? If you could put soccer in a bottle, I think it would be called NyQuil. Soccer on TV is like that old video game Pong. 'BOOOP . . . BOOOP . . . BOOOP.' Now leave us alone, Bruce, and write when you score again." Quacks were still patting themselves on the back for having no idea of what soccer was about back then. Amazing how much things have changed in a generation, with every sports bar showing soccer regularly in jumbo high def. Estimates put the worldwide total of soccer fans at 3.5 billion, and even in the United States we've come a long way. According to a Gallup Poll released in January 2018, soccer has now nearly surpassed baseball as the third-most popular US sport, with 7 percent calling it their favorite sport (third place), compared to 9 percent for baseball, that sport's lowest mark ever in the poll, which dates back to 1937, and 11 percent for basketball. Among eighteen- to thirty-four-year-olds, soccer actually ranked second behind only football, tied with basketball, each one chosen by 11 percent as their favorite sport—almost twice as popular in that age group as baseball, which was chosen by only 6 percent.

We lost to Argentina, 3–1, in our first game of the Olympics before a crowd of 83,183 at Legion Field in Birmingham but were able to bounce back two days later and score twice to beat Tunisia, 2–0. That set up a big game against Portugal at RFK Stadium in Washington, home field for DC United. We had a sellout crowd of 58,012, the largest ever for a sporting event at RFK up to that point, and we had our fate in our own hands—if we won, we'd make history by becoming the first US team to advance out of the first round of the Olympic soccer competition. For me that meant we were right where we wanted to be. "Our whole goal all along was to be able to get into Washington DC with the opportunity to advance," I told the *Washington Post*. "We have control of our destiny."

Portugal took an early 1–0 lead and we spent most of the game throwing everything we had at them. We had a 21–10 edge in shots and 16–6 in corners, but not until the seventy-fifth minute were we finally able to connect, making it 1–1 when midfielder Brian Maisonneuve scored off an A. J. Wood cross. The game ended with a flurry of action.

"So with last night's Olympic men's soccer match even and a jam-packed crowd at RFK Stadium standing and screaming, the United States put four years of preparation and seven months of training into a frenzied scoring effort in the last fifteen minutes," Steven Goff wrote in the *Washington Post*. "Shots skidded excruciatingly wide of Portugal's net, headers zipped over the crossbar and crossing passes went untouched. And when referee Edward Lennie's whistle sounded for the final time, the Americans' Olympic journey had come to a heartbreaking end." We were spent and devastated. Quotes from opposing coaches who have beaten you never make you feel any less bad, but I'll tip my cap to Nelo Vingada, the Portuguese coach: "It was a match of men," he said. "I must say, a great team is out." Thanks, Nelo.

We'd been tantalizingly close to doing something special but had fallen short. It felt good to be back with DC United and to be able to focus solely on one team. We were still finding our way, and I'm not going to deny I was steamed after we lost twice in five days to the Kansas City Wiz at the start of August. "It was a horrible display of defending," I said. "Just bad mistakes, bad decisions."

We finished the regular season 16-16, and traveled to the New York area to open the postseason against the MetroStars in East Rutherford, New Jersey, on a rainy day. Once again, I'll let Steven Goff of the *Washington Post* memorialize the occasion: "In an incredibly bizarre start to the Major League Soccer playoffs tonight, the New York/New Jersey MetroStars defeated D.C. United in the eleventh round of a controversial shootout in which Commissioner Doug Logan admitted 'the referee made a mistake.' The result still was in question nearly an hour after play had ended on Peter Vermes' goal, which seemingly gave the MetroStars a clinching, 6–5 edge in the shootout."

It was a joke! They went out of order. No way that result should have gone into the books, but once it did, let's just say we were one fired-up team moving forward. We won our next two games against the MetroStars, and won two straight in the Eastern Conference finals against Tampa Bay to set up a showdown with the LA Galaxy in the first MLS Cup. That was some game, played on a cold day at Foxboro Stadium in Massachusetts in the middle of an unbelievable storm. It just dumped rain. There were standing puddles on the field. It was a mud bowl out there, which made what happened all the more improbable. We fell behind in the fifth minute, and then early in the second half the Galaxy scored again to take a 2–0 lead. I did my best to stay confident on the sideline. We can get one back, I was telling everyone. But you just can't fall behind by two goals in a final. The odds are too much against ever making a game of it.

I loved that bunch of guys. They had spirit—and showed it that day. Three minutes after the Galaxy scored their second goal, I subbed in midfielder Tony Sanneh and then added Shawn Medved, another midfielder, in the seventieth minute. My plan was simple: get some balls in front of the goal. In those kind of conditions, anything could happen. We wore them down and started getting some good chances. Then in the seventy-third minute, Tony used his height and leaping ability to go up and get Marco Etcheverry's long free kick and head it home for our first goal. Nine minutes later, off of another Etcheverry free kick, it was Medved who scored, and we had a tie game. Once it went to sudden-death overtime, I was very confident of our chances. The Galaxy were stunned that they hadn't put us away. Etcheverry was the man again, launching a perfect corner kick, which Eddie

Pope headed into the goal. It was the kind of sports drama you see recorded in documentaries. Twenty-two years later, many still consider it the greatest MLS Cup.

"The Foxboro Stadium playing surface had turned into a muddy bog from the nor'easter that had punished the region all day," Steven Goff wrote in the *Washington Post*. "But in an improbable finish that American professional leagues with decades of history surely would envy, United charged back to tie the Major League Soccer championship match in regulation, then won it on twenty-two-year-old defender Eddie Pope's header in the fourth minute of sudden-death overtime for a 3–2 victory over the Los Angeles Galaxy. An infant season that began with the United losing six of seven games concluded with players and coaches, drenched to the bone, dancing deliriously and screaming for all of New England to hear. At the moment Pope's header settled into the net, the fifty-four-degree temperature, the thirty- to fifty-mph winds and the four inches of rain that had fallen didn't seem to matter a bit."

Part II

Breakthrough at the World Cup

National Team Coach

The 1998 World Cup in France was a disaster for the US team. Everyone had an opinion afterward on what went wrong, and I did, too, but one thing I've learned from my years of working with teams from the inside out is this: if you're not there, you don't know. If you're not part of a team, you're just guessing at what happened and why. But the blunt truth is, they just weren't a very good team. They had some talented players, but never really clicked as a team.

I think in some ways, the heady days of the 1994 World Cup, hosted by the US, set up some players for a fall. There was so much excitement, and US players landed good contracts and endorsement deals. They might have been pampered a little. Going into '98, the team had a lot of players used to being treated very well. Not everyone was going to be happy. It put the coach, Steve Sampson, in a difficult position. He had taken over after Bora Milutinović stepped down following the '94 Cup and had led the team to a strong fourth-place finish in Copa América 1995, but problems multiplied. The team was a mess going into the '98 World Cup, and stories emerged later from behind the scenes.

Kevin Payne, an influential figure as president of DC United and US Soccer, remembers raising a red flag in October 1997, the year before the World Cup. The US team was playing at RFK Stadium against Jamaica in one of its last World Cup qualifying games and looked ragged. They would have lost except that Eric Wynalda was able to sell the referee on a questionable penalty call and convert the kick to make it a 1–1 tie. Kevin met the next day with Alan Rothenberg and Sunil Gulati of US Soccer.

"I think you guys should make a change as soon as qualifying is over," Kevin remembers telling them. "I don't think this is going to work. You need a different coach. The time to make the change is before we go to France. You have a choice. We don't want to go to France and have a poor performance and *then* make the change."

They were listening.

"If we did that, then who would we hire?" Alan asked.

"It's very obvious that Bruce is the best American coach," Kevin said.

Looking back now, Alan agrees with that account. He said they all agreed that I was the best US coach and the only question was whether to hire an international coach or someone from the US. Sampson had been hired as an interim, and the timing on making a change was also awkward.

DC United opened the conference semifinals that year with a 4–1 home win over the New England Revolution the same day as the US 1–1 tie with Jamaica, then three days later were going to play the Revolution again at Foxboro. The day after the Jamaica game, Wynalda was dealing with an injury and came in to DC United to rehab. Apparently he was sitting there in the training room when I gave a speech to my guys next door in the team meeting room to get them fired up for our next playoff game.

"We're going to jump on New England from the opening whistle!" I said. "We're going to pressure them all over the field! They are never going to feel good about this game!"

Eric heard me hammer that point home a few times, and then called Kevin Payne over so he could tell him something.

"That's what we needed to hear before our match with Jamaica," Kevin remembers Eric telling him. "This is the guy who should be our coach."

I don't know if making a coaching change at that point then would have helped much. Things couldn't have gone much worse in France. The US lost all three of its games, first to Germany, 2–0, the second goal coming from a German striker named Jürgen Klinsmann, then to Iran and Yugoslavia. The high hopes of two years earlier had been dashed. "For one reason or another, this whole thing was a shambles," Tab Ramos said afterward.

The great *New York Times* columnist George Vecsey, writing from France, was a little sarcastic in summing up the US flop. "Of course, it is hard for strikers to function in Sampson's 3-6-1 formation, which leaves one forward as isolated as the frontier scout played by Kevin Costner in the movie 'Dances With Wolves,'" Vecsey wrote.

George was not persuaded by Alan Rothenberg's take on what happened in France. "Rothenberg noted that the United States had played three losses in 1990, and achieved a second-round loss to Brazil in 1994," he wrote. "He insisted this year's three-and-out performance was in some ways an improvement. He must have been watching Nigeria or Mexico. The United States team basically could not pass or shoot. To their credit, however, the lads did qualify for France, which allowed hundreds of Americans to wander around this lovely Loire Estuary town, happily eating crustaceans and wearing their Sam's Army T-shirts."

Steve Sampson resigned within days after the World Cup. "Three losses is not an acceptable result," he told the *San Diego Union-Tribune*. "Maybe it's time for someone else to see what they can do."

My time had come. I was contacted literally just after the World

Cup, that June, and had a good idea that I'd be taking over the US team later that year. That was in the middle of the DC United season and I was under contract, so US Soccer would have to work out the details with Kevin Payne of getting me out of my contract if they were going to hire me.

In August we all headed down to Florida for the MLS All-Star Game at the Citrus Bowl in Orlando. The game itself was far more interesting than all-star games usually are. That was the year a new format was introduced: the game featured one side made up of foreign MLS players and the other of US players. Usually all-star games are at least somewhat halfhearted. Guys don't play with much intensity. That game in Orlando was something else completely. The US players were still seething over the World Cup; it was very fresh, the feeling of having been ridiculed and humiliated for falling so far short of expectations, especially their own, and finishing dead-last in the tournament. I didn't concern myself with that part at all. As the coach of an all-star team, you just put your team together, keep them loose, and let them enjoy the event. I didn't make it a personal thing by any means, but they played as though they were on a mission. We jumped out to a quick 3–0 lead in the first sixteen minutes on goals by Tab Ramos, Alexi Lalas, and Brian McBride and went on to win 6–1.

"This proves to the skeptics that Americans can play," McBride said afterward.

The headline in the *New York Times* was "Americans Play like a Team," which seemed to suggest a response of "Finally!"

I wanted a shot at coaching the Olympic team and thought I'd earned the job. I'd won seven national championships by then, five at Virginia and two with DC United; players I'd coached formed a core of talent we'd need to rely on moving forward, and I was tired of what I saw as an inferiority complex about US talent, including coaching talent. Down in Orlando for the all-star game, I went to see Alan Rothenberg at his suite in the Peabody

Hotel, the one where they used to have ducks marching in the lobby fountain every day. It was a two-hour job interview—and it went very well. I came out of there feeling that I had the job.

Speculation was running that US Soccer might hire another European, maybe even bringing back Bora Milutinović again. Alex Yannis even did an article in the *Times* that August, two days after the MLS All-Star Game, claiming that Bora "appears to be the front-runner to coach the American team again," and added that among the four candidates to succeed Sampson, I appeared to rank last in Rothenberg's preference—behind Bora, the Brazilian Carlos Alberto Parreira, and Carlos Queiroz of Portugal. That was old information.

"I love Bora and I still love Bora, but no, by that time he was out of it," Alan recalls.

Alan's term was up and he was handing his responsibilities over to a new president, Bob Contiguglia, who ended up being named on August 22. "Bob felt strongly that he wanted an American coach," Kevin recalls. "I kept saying, 'Bruce is the right guy. He understands the American player. He knows who the best players are and he communicates best with them.'" In the end they reached a consensus. "Bob and Sunil and Hank and I all talked about it and agreed it should be Bruce," Alan recalls.

An announcement finally came just after the MLS Cup, which we ended up losing 2–0 to the Chicago Fire, coached by Bob Bradley. We'd gone into the final confident, looking for our third straight championship, and Bob's team did a hell of a job against us. Press accounts were on the breathless side, but it was a surprising result. "Sunday's crushing 2–0 loss to the expansion Fire in MLS Cup '98 before 51,350 at the Rose Bowl was something two-time champion United was simply not prepared for," *USA Today*'s Peter Brewington wrote. "The result was one of the bigger upsets in Major League Soccer's three-year history." Brewington was right. You're never prepared to lose the big ones. You have to go into the game expecting to win. That loss stung, but I was excited to get right to work for the US national team.

Once again, it was out to San Jose, California, for my first game coaching the national side, a friendly with Australia. There was a wave of optimism about the future that went with me taking over, and I knew it would last only as long as we showed clear signs of progress. Job one was developing young talent, the point I emphasized at every turn. Out in California getting ready for the game, the youth-movement theme was so overworked, I joked, "Maybe we should get the toys out." *USA Today* ran a headline: "America Thinks Young for Australia Game."

I had a lot to learn about coaching at the top level. I was getting on-the-job training, which I needed. Experience is everything for a coach, and if you haven't coached at the international level before, it's a jarring transition. You're basically in a Catch-22 situation, since you need time to acquire the experience that gives your judgment the grounding it needs in real-life realities, but without the experience you might not be able to survive long enough to *get* the experience. Back then it was different, though. I came in at a time when there was interest and excitement but expectations of immediate success were fairly low. The sport was still in its infancy here in the US, so you weren't being scrutinized the way you are now. Back then, I could learn from my mistakes, which was how you move forward, but now it would be much harder. Expectations and scrutiny have both taken a giant leap forward. Today, no one is ever happy about anything we do. That's just the way it is. Which is good. That's what you want. It's like the difference between running a baseball team in a Sun Belt city where people are just happy to have the big leagues in town, and being the guy in New York or Boston and knowing that you're going to be both second-guessed and celebrated at every turn. That was what I always wanted for US soccer and that's where we are now.

I'd compare my experiences back then to taking a trip with

no map and no clear idea of the landscape. I was flying blind. I made mistakes at every turn. To plan for international competitions, you need to have a detailed understanding of what the international game is and how it's different than the soccer I'd coached up until then. You have to know your region, each of the teams, how you will go about beating them and which players you need to do that. You have to learn how to spot players who can make the jump to international competition, which is faster and more intense. Some very good players at the club level don't make the jump to international competition, for whatever reason, and it takes years to develop insights into the hows and whys of that. Back then you also had to develop a persistence in what you could call the politics of fielding a strong team nationally, always pushing for growth in the level of funding, a shoestring budget compared to how it is now. You needed to learn about reaching out to different constituencies and having them involved and energized in moving US soccer forward. I'm the first to say that in my early years as US national coach, I had a steep learning curve.

I started my tenure as coach with what I can only call a bad game. I'm sure for college football, Spartan Stadium is an excellent venue. They've always had great fans, going back to the days when a guy named Crazy George would rev them up by banging on a little drum. For soccer it was a terrible stadium, and that was an awful game. "There was little for an announced crowd of 15,074 to cheer about," the San Jose paper wrote, and I'd say that was, if anything, an understatement. About all I could say after my first game with a new group of players was: "We know we have a lot of work to do."

I said after that game that we hoped the team would improve once we had Claudio Reyna back to nail down the midfield. He was playing over in Germany at the time of the Australia game, but we did look better when we had him and some others who played in Europe. By the following February, we felt better about ourselves. We took on Germany in Jacksonville, Florida, in a friendly that the Germans were sure they'd win. They chartered a plane and brought maybe a hundred journalists along, and then we just spanked them from the start. It was a classic game in the US playing on a field that was a little short, and a little narrow, but we played very well and won 3–0. We knew people would write it off as just a friendly, but it meant a lot to us, beating a side that had already at that point won three world championships.

"Are the Tectonic Plates Shifting? U.S. Beats Germany," ran the headline in the *New York Times*.

"Today's result will be a surprise around the world," I said at the time. "It's not surprising in our locker room."

All three of the goals were scored by players who were with teams in Germany at the time. It might not have been Germany's best day, but they had Oliver Kahn as their goalkeeper, so to beat Germany you always had to earn it.

"In the twenty-fourth minute, midfielder Tony Sanneh electrified the partisan crowd with a breakaway," Jack Bell wrote in the *Times*. "He outmaneuvered German midfielder Jens Jeremies for the loose ball and zeroed in on Kahn. The goalie burst toward him to limit his angle, but Sanneh slipped a shot by him on the left."

It was just one small step in the direction that we needed to go, but an important one. Cobi Jones spoke for many when he said, "Our attitude was 'Take no prisoners!'" showing that our efforts to jack up the team's confidence had been yielding some results.

We had another shot at Germany five months later at the Confederations Cup in Mexico and stunned them again, this time 2–0, to knock them out of the tournament. I was proud of the way we played, especially with a lineup featuring some new faces, but I remember thinking at the time that it didn't seem that the Germans had much interest in playing in the Confederations Cup. Their captain, Lothar Matthäus, looked as though he had

no interest in playing that day. There was one play at the end of
the first half where Matthäus, FIFA World Player of the Year for
1991, made a move on goal from the top of the penalty area and
Ben Olsen ran him down and shouldered him off the ball, and
that was about all we heard from Lothar for the rest of the day.
That game was in Guadalajara, which is another mile-high city,
like Denver (at 5,138 feet), and the Germans looked out of gas.
The win over Germany earned us a trip to Mexico City and a
semifinal matchup against Mexico at the Estadio Azteca, all the
way up at 7,382 feet, and even after training for two and a half
weeks, the altitude at Azteca still wore us down. If we'd won it in
regulation, we might have been all right, but it was tied through
ninety minutes, and in added time we just died. It showed how
really hard it is to get a team to adjust to those extreme conditions. Mexico won it on Cuauhtémoc Blanco's Golden Goal six
minutes into overtime, and we were on our way to the third-place
game, which we won. We had something to show for our work
and knew we were making progress, which was encouraging for
the program.

"As early as Arena's third match in charge, the wounds suffered at France 98 began to heal," Dave Wangerin wrote in *Soccer in a Football World: The Story of America's Forgotten Game*,
published in 2006 in England. "In February 1999 the U.S. beat
Germany 3–0 in a friendly in Jacksonville, Florida, a surprising
result magnified by the fact that all three goals were scored by
Germany-based players (and) . . . six months later, at the Confederations Cup in Mexico, Arena beat the Germans again with
almost a reserve squad."

I still had a lot to learn. No progress we made would really matter that much unless we could improve on the disastrous World
Cup performance of the US team in France. Nothing is worse than
getting your players fired up and confident, only to put them in
a position to fail. That's how you crush confidence and belief.

You want them confident and prepared to pull off the achievable, so they can build on one success. Everything we were working on with the team could move forward only with important wins along the way to set a tone and add weight to our ideas. The work was still daunting, but it was starting to get fun.

Landon

Talented teenagers have to make a lot of progress before they really show up on my radar. It's not that I'm skeptical about their futures; it's really just a question of being a realist. A lot of talented kids come along; I'm always hearing about the latest young guy someone is excited about, but most of the time those kids don't pan out, for one reason or another. You think of a guy like Freddy Adu—talented kid, good family, everything going for him, but it never happened for him anything like the way everyone wanted it to happen.

Landon Donovan was not on my radar while he was a youngster making a name for himself in Southern California. He grew up an hour east of LA in a community called Redlands, near where the desert runs into the San Bernardino Mountains. His father was a former hockey player, a Canadian, but his parents were divorced when he was only two, and Landon, his twin sister, Tristan, and their older brother, Josh, were raised by their mother, Donna Kenney-Cash, a special education specialist at Porter Elementary School in nearby Fontana. To handle an exhausting job like that and raise three small children, that takes a lot—and her example inspired Landon. "A lot of times when I would get exhausted, I'd think about my mother and how hard she worked," he remembers.

Landon could have been great in anything he did, in academics or athletics. He's very bright and he's a great soccer player but an even greater person, which is saying a lot. I think that has a lot to do with his upbringing. He was a natural athlete from the beginning and was running by the time he was about twelve months. He also learned early about responsibility. His mother had him doing his own laundry from the age of six, just like his sister and older brother, taking his turn washing dishes and mowing the lawn. "Part of it was, she wanted us to learn to do things on our own, and part of it was, she just didn't have time," Landon says.

I first saw Landon play in Bradenton, Florida. Landon was recruited into the US Soccer U-17 Residency Program, and we took DC United, the reigning MLS champion at the time, down to Florida for preseason training, which included a game against the U-17s. Landon was fifteen at the time, talented but brash. He was running around the field shooting his mouth off, like a lot of cocky young kids that age, and we noticed. "For the DC United guys it was a preseason game and they didn't want to be out there," Landon remembers now. "But for us, we were playing an MLS team! This was the coolest thing ever! We were being little pricks out there and I could sense in the way they were reacting and responding that they wanted to beat the shit out of these little kids."

He has that right. I remember thinking, *If I was one of the players out on the field in that game, I would have probably tried to kick him up in the air!* At the same time, I was very impressed with Landon. Then they went on and had a very good under-seventeen World Cup, and Landon was named the best player in the tournament. I knew he was special, but I wasn't going to gush over him.

Landon was always a student of the game. He had a great feel for what was happening around him, and he always tried to get better. John Ellinger, his coach on the US under-seventeen team, remembers one time in France in 1997 when he showed his players a highlight reel of Ronaldo, the great Brazilian. Afterward, one player came up and asked to see the video again: Landon, who was sixteen, making his first international trip. The next day, Landon scored the game winner against New Zealand, using a move he skillfully copied from Ronaldo.

"I remember watching that film," Landon says now. "I was a player that liked to use my speed and get in behind defenses, so I ended up getting on a lot of breakaways and would be one-on-one with the goalkeeper. What that tape showed me is, when you got there, you could actually dribble around the goalkeeper, which had never occurred to me. The next day, I did that. It wasn't that difficult technically. I think it says a lot about coach Ellingner that he wanted to show us that tape, which had an immediate impact on me. I was able to internalize it."

Even by mid-1999, after Landon had signed a four-year deal with Bayer Leverkusen of the Bundesliga, and was earning poetic praise in the press, I was holding off on too many compliments. Jack Bell wrote in the *New York Times* in May 1999 about Landon being both a "goal poacher and a goal creator," and added, "He has a keen sense of positioning beyond his years and an ability to see the game several moves ahead, like a chess grandmaster."

That article then quoted me, by then the coach of the men's national team: "For his age, from what I've seen, I think he's a good player with a lot of potential. He certainly needs to get more high-level games before we know for sure. . . . I will say that I think there is a bit too much being said about him already. He needs time to develop as a player and as a person."

I don't think we do kids any favors when we build them up before they've had a chance to become who they are going to be.

I've said this again and again: people have a hard time understanding, but just because a player is outstanding at fifteen or sixteen or seventeen does not mean he will turn into a top-flight player at twenty. It's one kind of special to show you have the talent to make people see your future, and another kind of special to learn enough along the way to turn that potential into the complete package.

I named Landon to our eighteen-man roster going into our national team friendly with Argentina in June 1999, so we could bring him to camp and let him get his feet wet. He was only seventeen. I didn't think he would cap. We had seven European-based players available, putting us in a good position to field a strong lineup. I just wanted Landon to be around for a camp and soak up a sense of how you go about preparing for international competition. You have to take the long view, and it was important to think about Landon's development.

Here's how he remembers it, and feel free to take his praise with a grain of salt. I know I do! "My first real encounter with Bruce was when I was seventeen and he brought me in to a camp just to get a feel for it," Landon recalls. "A lot of other coaches, especially at that time in US soccer, would say, 'Oh he's talented! Let's bring him in and throw him into the fire!' One of Bruce's best attributes is that he puts people in a position to succeed. You have one of three ways. You can just put people out there thoughtlessly, you can put people in a position where there's a very high likelihood they're going to succeed, or you put them in a position where they're likely to fail. Bruce is an expert in putting people in a position where they're going to succeed, and not just players, but staff and everyone around him."

We won that game against Argentina 1–0. Landon watched the whole thing from the bench and was in the raucous locker room afterward. That was a year of adjustment for him, going off to Germany, an experience he looks back on now with mixed feelings. "In some ways it was hard, and in some ways it was incredible," he says, smiling. "I got to play every day with guys who in almost every case were better than me and pushed me. I was learning so much. They would take time with me to develop me and help me get better. Initially, it was very exciting. I loved being on my own. Imagine, being sixteen, and a pretty independent kid as it was, getting a chance to do whatever you wanted, with no homework. It was kind of a dream come true in that way. I could sit on the couch watching TV and eating cereal."

If it had worked out to where he was getting regular playing time, the hard parts of the transition to playing in Germany would have been less challenging. "Eventually when I wasn't playing, it started to wear on me," he says. "I was there to play, and I wanted to go somewhere I could play. If I'd been playing every game and life was great and I was scoring and popular, all those things can mask a lot. But when that wasn't happening either, that made it difficult. I missed California. I was homesick for everything, the weather, the lifestyle, the food, my family, my friends, all that. I remember once toward the end when I was pretty homesick, flying all the way from Germany to California to see my family and friends for one day. I was home for sixteen hours total, and then I got on a plane to fly back."

Landon did well when he played for the United States, earning the Golden Boot as MVP of the US under-seventeen World Cup team in New Zealand in 1999, but his style was not always a good fit for the Bundesliga. "They just had no use for my style of soccer—not at that age, not from a kid who hadn't proven anything," Landon told *Sports Illustrated*. "That was the only way I knew how to play. I was never taught to keep my mouth shut. I was never taught to just work hard and wait my time."

Even if Landon's time playing for Bayer Leverkusen's reserve team fell short of what it could have been, still he was gaining experience. We knew he was close to being ready to make a mark with the national team. It's a delicate balance between thinking of the kid and his future and wanting to take advantage of what he can do for your team. In July 2000, we had to go down to Guatemala for our first qualifying game leading toward the 2002 World Cup, and we were dealing with injuries to Jeff Agoos, Ben Olsen, and Eddie Pope. For some reason, the game was played in Mazatenango, an out-of-the-way town of forty thousand people located in the low-lying jungle of western Guatemala, toward Mexico. I might have liked to have Landon in that game, but a road World Cup qualifying game under those circumstances would not have been an ideal setting for him to excel. I remember, about eight thousand people showed up for the game. The night before, loud music was blasting right outside our two-star motel for most of the night, making it hard to get much sleep. We woke up to another hot and humid day.

We had a strong first half and took a 1–0 lead, then had a tough second half, with Guatemala's Carlos Ruiz scoring on a questionable play in the eighty-eighth minute after fouling US defender Carlos Llamosa in the penalty area. We had to settle for one point in a game we should have won. I wasn't happy. Jamie Trecker of the *New York Times* called it a "shocking result" and a "disastrous start" to World Cup qualifying in an article that described me this way: "Bruce Arena, soaked to the skin by the oppressive humidity of the Guatemalan jungle, looked like a man with a bad migraine." It was miserably hot that day, that's for sure.

"Like it or not," the article continued, "the United States has not been able to develop a new cadre of young players inside the country—in fact, one could be excused for doing a double-take Sunday as the aging Tab Ramos made an appearance as a second-half sub. In many ways, this team is essentially unchanged from the squad that finished a humiliating last in France in 1998. Major League Soccer is still not a factor—the international game is a much faster, tougher brand than the fairly weak brew that the

American league serves up. . . . Landon Donovan, who has been stellar for the Olympic squad after under-17 World Cup stardom, is a quality finisher for the future but is also unseasoned."

Some coaches also worried about Landon's small stature. The coach of the US Olympic team that year, Clive Charles, held Landon out of the first two US games in the Sydney Olympics that summer, worried that he'd get beaten up. Landon admitted later he was disappointed, then kicked himself and told himself, *Quit being a baby.* Finally in the third game, he came off the bench and scored one goal in the 3–1 win.

Here's how *Times* columnist George Vecsey described what happened: "Tonight's game began in a driving rain, and Charles's own college player, Conor Casey, a strapping forward, had trouble planting his thick legs and moving his thick trunk. He was flopping all over the wet grounds, as Charles displayed either genius or overdue common sense—depending on which chat room you are reading—and sent Donovan into the game in the thirtieth minute tonight. He promptly kick-started the United States squad from a stolid state into something approximating fluidity and grace and intuition, all extremely un-American."

Landon scored another goal in the US win over Japan in the quarterfinals, and one more win would have given the US its first Olympic medal in men's soccer since 1904, but the team lost to Spain and then Chile and had to settle for fourth place.

Looking at the schedule, I knew that an October 26 friendly at the Coliseum in Los Angeles might be a good place for Landon to make his first appearance with the national team, even if the opponent happened to be Mexico, always a tough challenge. He'd shown some progress when I saw him in camp. The guys on the US Olympic team had a great time making sure he wasn't too taken with the hype and kept mocking him as a "superstar." He took it all in good spirit. He was not a starter, but Chris Henderson went down with an injury, so I walked down the bench.

"Landon, warm up," I said.

He looked up at me blankly for a second. His cleats weren't even tied. Then he warmed up, and I sent him into the game. He got the ball on a breakaway in the second half, skipped past the Mexican goalkeeper, and then punched it home for a goal. Later he set up our second goal as well, and we won 2–0.

Landon's time was coming. He spoke to his agent, Richard Motzkin, my agent as well, and asked if there was any way he could leave Germany and come play for a Major League Soccer team. He was tired of sitting on the bench. He needed to play and wanted to play. The San Jose Earthquakes and LA Galaxy were both very interested, but San Jose had first shot, and that was where Landon ended up, signing a four-year deal in March 2001 that brought him back to his home state of California. He didn't know where San Jose was and he didn't care. "When they said 'San Jose,' I didn't even know how far that was from LA," he recalled later. The move was good for Landon, and it was good for US soccer, which needed to have its young talent developing, not idling on the bench.

2002 World Cup

As a national-team coach trying to prepare your team to qualify for the World Cup, you have to be single-minded in your focus, but no one who lived through the 9/11 attacks of 2001 could think about much else for a while, especially no one from New York. The month of September 2001 started out bad for us with a stunning 3–2 loss to Honduras in a September 1 World Cup qualifying game, the first time in sixteen years that the US had lost a home World Cup qualifying game—and the first time in forty-one years we'd given up three goals in a home World Cup qualifier. Five days later we lost our third straight World Cup qualifying game 2–0 in San Jose, Costa Rica. The press said our "nightmare continues," words that rang hollow when the attacks came and we all learned new lessons about what a nightmare could look like.

I remember coming out of the shower as my wife told me there were reports of a plane hitting the World Trade Center. Then we heard about a plane crashing into the Pentagon, which hit close to home. We were only fifteen miles away in Fairfax, Virginia. Anyone old enough to remember that day will never forget seeing the terrible images on endless replay, first one of the World Trade Center towers crumbling after a hijacked plane slammed into it, then the other, then the attack on the Pentagon, and finally the wreckage of the fourth plane near Shanksville, Pennsylvania. For me, as for so many others, the loss was personal. My good friend Eamon McEneaney, a senior vice president at Cantor Fitzgerald whom I coached in freshman lacrosse at Cornell, was one among the nearly three thousand people killed that day in the terrorist attacks. Eamon was an amazing guy, small but tough. He was an attackman on the US team I played on that took second in the 1978 World Lacrosse Championships in England. Eamon came through one terrorist attack. He was a hero of the 1993 terrorist bombing of the World Trade Center when he saved the lives of sixty-three people. "They were hysterical, and he pulled them together and wet paper towels for them to put over their faces and made them form a human chain and took them down the stairs," his wife, Bonnie, recalled. I recall that when Eamon and Bonnie came down to Charlottesville to visit Phyllis and me, Eamon told me he was eager to finish up at Cantor and then retire, to get back to his original love: writing poetry. He was seriously considering moving to Charlottesville, where he could write poetry and coach lacrosse.

On October 7, the day of our World Cup qualifying game with Jamaica at Foxboro Stadium outside Boston, US and British aircraft started bombing Afghanistan, specifically targeting the Taliban and al Qaeda, starting a war in Afghanistan that basically continues to this day. I found out we were at war before the game and decided to tell the players. It only seemed right. I didn't elaborate, I just let them know we were bombing Afghanistan and they should know. The news did make the National Anthem more emotional than normal, but once that was behind us, it was game time and the players and coaching staff pushed away all other thoughts or concerns. Joe-Max Moore scored both goals in our

2–1 win, and just after the game we found out that Mexico and Costa Rica had played to a scoreless tie in their qualifying game, and somehow Trinidad and Tobago had scored an upset victory in Honduras, meaning we'd qualified for the World Cup! We had a nice celebration right there in the Foxboro end zone, which the crowd of more than forty thousand enjoyed. It had come down to the wire, but we were on our way to South Korea/Japan.

That December brought the draw, an important exercise that can determine the fate of any country in the World Cup. A small number of top soccer countries are so strong, they can fight through a tough draw, but for us, that was a long shot. We flew over to Pusan, South Korea, to be on hand when our fate was determined, and I'll put it this way: at least I wasn't cursing afterward. We were in a group with Portugal, South Korea, and Poland. To advance out of the group, we'd need a win and a tie, most likely. I knew Portgual would be a challenge. They were ranked fifth in the world, led by World Player of the Year Luís Figo; they had gone undefeated in qualifying, and many experts considered them a favorite to win their group and make a long run in the tournament. South Korea, as one of the host countries, would of course be a handful. In fact, in the history of the World Cup up until then, no host country had failed to advance out of its group. Poland was the first team to qualify out of Europe.

Above all, it was a sharp contrast with our dire draw four years earlier going into the World Cup in France. "Portugal, South Korea and Poland do not loom as menacingly as Germany, Yugoslavia and Iran did four years ago, before the Yanks finished thirty-second and last," *New York Times* columnist George Vecsey wrote. "They were done on the windy evening in Marseille when the names Germany, Yugoslavia and Iran popped up on the board. All three nations had, shall we say, a political history with the United States, but even more important were the soccer ramifications: two formidable European teams and one feisty outsider."

We started off 2002 by winning the Gold Cup, despite a shaky showing against South Korea in our first game, which we took 2–1 on a late goal from DaMarcus Beasley. Then it was the Brian McBride show. Two days later, back at the Rose Bowl, he scored on a penalty kick to give us a 1–0 win over Cuba. Then against El Salvador in the semifinal, he scored three goals in the space of twelve minutes, and we won 4–0. After a scoreless tie with Canada, which we won on kicks, we played our best game of the tournament in the final, dominating Costa Rica 2–0. For me it was a learning experience about the critical importance of coming together as a team and methodically preparing. "It's the first time in my three years that we really had a training camp and we saw it pay dividends," I said after the win. "If we can prepare for thirty-five days before Korea, we will put a good team on the field."

I gave a speech before a group of coaches that April in Seattle, and when someone asked me how I thought we would do against Portugal in our opening game, I didn't tap-dance. "I like the matchup a lot," I said, and I could see some of the coaches in the group thought I was just putting a good face on it. But I wasn't. I meant what I said. The assumption was that if we had a shot at getting through, we'd pick up our points against South Korea and Poland. Portugal was seen as too formidable. But the more I thought about it, looking beyond Figo and a few other talented attacking players, I thought Portugal had a suspect defense and a lack of speed that we could exploit.

I had my longtime assistant coach Glenn Myernick heading the team scouting our World Cup opponents, and Mooch took Portugal himself, following them around Europe during the spring of 2002. One time in April, Mooch ran into Figo at Lisbon Airport on his way back to join Real Madrid. He looked tired. "There's nothing more that I'd like than to get in the limo and go home and go to bed for three days," Figo told Mooch.

We felt we had an edge in preparation and athleticism. Basically, we had to mix up our defense a little to give us the best shot at stopping Portugal's attack, and make sure our backs just focused on defending. My other main concern was our many veterans, who were coming off such a dismal performance four years earlier in France. For Cobi Jones, Claudio Reyna, Joe-Max Moore, and Earnie Stewart, this was the third World Cup, and they'd won only one game in the first two, at home against Colombia in 1994. I didn't want them playing tentative, deliberate soccer. I wanted to see them going for it, playing loose and confident.

That was why we were fortunate to have Landon Donovan and DaMarcus Beasley on the team, two young players who brought a burst of energy to the field and never lacked for confidence. They'd been named the top two players of the 1999 world under-seventeen team, Landon winning the Golden Ball Award and DaMarcus winning the Silver Ball. I'd brought Landon along slowly and had a similar plan in mind with DaMarcus. The main thing was for him to be comfortable, so he could play his best and learn as much as possible.

"He made sure that I felt like part of the team," DaMarcus remembers. "It didn't matter how young you were; it didn't matter how inexperienced. If you were in camp, you were there for a reason. Everybody was equal, from our captain Claudio Reyna down to myself, being a young kid in his first camp. When you had that in your head from Bruce, I think that helped me be comfortable with the group, and just go out there and play, not think about anything else but playing football."

Once DaMarcus made the World Cup roster, we expected him to be in a reserve role, soaking up the experience and learning what was required, so that down the road he could be a major contributor. But in camp he kept impressing me. I loved his speed and his competitiveness and decided to start him against Portugal. I remember his reaction when I gave him the news.

"That's cool," he said, and walked away.

My toughest decision was who to start in goal. Kasey Keller and Brad Friedel were both good choices. I knew that both expected to play, and either would be pissed off if asked to sit on the bench, but I also knew they'd keep that frustration to themselves and not make an issue of it that could prove disruptive. I gave the nod to Brad, who'd had a great season for the Blackburn Rovers of the English Premier League. His strong kicking game would help us bring the attack to Portugal. Brad could strike the ball seventy yards on a rope and connect with McBride time and time again. We wanted to pressure Portugal in their defensive half of the field whenever possible.

It might be too much to say Portugal was looking past us, but we knew they didn't devote much time to preparing for us as their first opponent. They were confident they could handle us with relative ease. Our guys were confident, too—from the most experienced to the least.

"That was my first World Cup, and I remember everything about that day starting with walking out in the tunnel," says Da-Marcus Beasley now. "You're seeing Luís Figo, you're seeing Sérgio Conceição, you're seeing all these big players, and it's like, *I'm twenty years old!* Myself and Landon, we were looking at each other, taking it all in. But one thing I'll never forget is right before we had our pregame meal, Earnie Stewart told me, 'Beez, just play.' And then he walked away. So that was it. But those couple words helped get me through that game and just play."

I remember just before the game when they came off the field and gathered in our locker room twenty minutes before kickoff, I liked what I saw. They did not look tight or overwhelmed. I saw a look of confidence in their faces. We went over what we'd been talking about for six months, an aggressive approach to take advantage of our athleticism and speed.

"When we win today, I'm not going to be surprised," I told

them. "First tackle today, first foul, first shot, first goal," I repeated.

"You represent the greatest country in the world," I told the guys. "Have a lot of pride."

For all of us, so soon after September 11, those words carried added importance and meaning. Our game plan was to take the attack to Portugal from the get-go—and that was just what we did. Four minutes in, we earned a corner kick, and the rebound bounced to John O'Brien, who converted. John's goal put Portugal on their heels and was as important as any we scored in the competition. We made it 2–0 in the twenty-ninth minute when a Landon cross glanced off defender Jorge Costa and found the net, getting past goalkeeper Vítor Baía. "I was watching, watching, watching and saying, 'Oh my God, it's going in,'" Landon said later. Lucky? Absolutely, but when you're working hard and dictating the action, often you make your own luck.

One of our best players in the game was Tony Sanneh, who did a great job on Figo and helped us take a 3–0 lead. "By this time, Sanneh . . . had neutralized the ornate midfielder Luis Figo, the reigning world player of the year," Jere Longman wrote in the *New York Times*. "Still not fully recovered from an ankle injury, Figo appeared completely lacking in energy and artistry. It was Sanneh instead who found his creative side with a cross from the right flank that would have made David Beckham envious. The ball traveled forty yards, bending perfectly onto the head of McBride at the far post. Baia was caught out of position again, and McBride put the Americans ahead by an astonishing 3–0."

We had to sweat it out in the second half. We gave up a goal just before halftime on a corner. Even when Portugal cut the lead to 3-2 on an own goal in the seventy-first minute, an unfortunate moment for Jeff Agoos, I still felt we were in control of the game. We were fit, we were mentally focused, and we had the mix of experience and young talent to make the most of our advantage. We even pressed the attack, with DaMarcus using his explosive speed to make smart runs and Landon and Cobi Jones joining in when they could. We held on. To the world, I'm sure our 3–2 victory over Portugal was shocking. No one in our locker room was shocked at all.

"We're there!" a giddy Bob Contiguglia, president of US Soccer, said afterward. "We've shown we can play with anyone in the world."

Bob, a kidney specialist in his fifties, looked like a happy kid afterward in our locker room, with Cobi Jones showing him how to do a victory dance. Many were calling it the most important win for the US in the World Cup since we beat England in Brazil back in 1950, more than half a century earlier, but I called it three points and time to move on. I was already thinking about how we'd handle the South Koreans, helped by all that goes into a home-field advantage. We wanted to win, but knew that a tie— and the one point it would give us—might be enough for us to advance.

It's always tough in sports to win on the road, whether you're the Yankees going into Fenway Park and all that the Boston fans dish out or any team playing the Golden State Warriors at home. I'm going to go out on a limb and say that what we faced in Daegu that day, playing in front of a delirious crowd of more than sixty thousand people, amounted to one of the most lopsided home-field advantages in the history of sports. The entire country basically came to a halt so every South Korean could focus on our game. The result was critical for both sides. The game was in the hottest and most humid part of the country, which was one more advantage for the South Koreans, known as the fittest team in the entire tournament. Throw in an undercurrent of deep resentment, with a whole country whipped up against the US, outraged that a South Korean speed skater was stripped of his gold medal at the Salt Lake City Olympics after a review led officials to conclude that he had interfered with American Apolo Anton Ohno, who was awarded the medal. It was a volatile mix.

We were used to dealing with challenges on the road. A local radio station in Panama had parked a flatbed truck in front of our team hotel, loaded up with huge speakers, and blasted loud music all night long, so we could hardly sleep. After the game, there were no operable showers—and we had a plane to catch, so players doused themselves with bottled water. DaMarcus Beasley lined up to take a corner kick in El Salvador one time and had half a chicken thrown at him. He didn't say which half. In Costa Rica, players had been pelted with coins, batteries, and bags of urine.

Dave Sarachan had been in charge of scouting South Korea and had done his usual thorough job, but when it came to the team meeting to brief the guys on what to expect, I pretty much had to throw up my hands. They had so many guys named Lee or Kim, it didn't make too much sense to keep repeating the same names.

"To hell with this," I said. "They've got a bunch of really fast, fit guys that run all over the damned place. They've got Lees and Kims all over the field. You better be ready to battle!"

I'd held Clint Mathis out of the Portugal game because fitness in that game was going to be crucial, and he just wasn't fit enough, but I started him against South Korea. He was probably our best finisher, and I had a hunch he might deliver, even if he couldn't give us ninety minutes. Clint was a media darling who had appeared on the cover of *Sports Illustrated*, and some thought it was surprising I'd sat him earlier. He showed his value against South Korea, scoring a brilliant goal in the twenty-fourth minute off a great pass from John O'Brien. Brad Friedel had another strong game for us in goal, stopping a penalty shot and a shot from ten yards out early in the second half. The equalizer came in the seventy-eighth minute, and South Korea probably should have won, but we held on for the 1–1 tie and one critical point. South Korea outshot us 19–6, and Choi Yong-soo missed a point-blank shot in the ninetieth minute. Teams that get through always need a little luck here and there.

"We didn't only play against the Korean team," I said afterward, "we played against a nation today."

Something wasn't right going into our game against Poland. In our last practice, guys were taking home videos and pictures for their scrapbooks. They looked like a bunch of damned tourists, not a team preparing for a game against a powerful opponent. We arrived at the stadium for the game, and our guys were talking to the players from Poland, all chummy-chummy, which I hate. Our mind-set was a long way from right, I realized, but by then there was not a lot to do about that. For the Polish players, all pressure was off. They'd lost their first two games and were going home the next day, no matter what. They were loose. They drilled us, 3–1, a loss that would have been devastating but for the fact that South Korea somehow beat Portugal and we had advanced out of our group. Next up: our arch rival, Mexico.

Back then I was hard on the Mexicans for the way they handled getting beaten by us, 2–0, on goals by Brian McBride and Landon Donovan. They hit us with cheap shots all over the field, and it seemed that Cobi Jones had a bull's-eye on his back over the last twenty minutes. They became the first team I'd ever seen in the World Cup that did not exchange jerseys afterward in the universal gesture of good sportsmanship. For them, losing to the *norteamericanos* was too humiliating to bear. They saw soccer as *their* sport, a realm where they always had an edge over their rivals to the north, and our totally outplaying them was hard for them to take. Then, even after both teams had climbed onto their buses to leave, there was a delay, and we both sat there for what felt like a long time. The Mexicans were all fuming. Our guys were drinking beers and cheering. It might only have been ten minutes, but those were ten sweet minutes for us. That game was massive in terms of growing the rivalry. The newspaper reports out of Mexico talked as if the world had ended.

We knew we were going to play Germany tough. The Germans were one of the great world soccer powers, having won the World Cup three times already at that point, but we'd beaten them twice in my first year as coach and we didn't fear them. Our goals going into the World Cup were to play as a team, to play hard, to establish a clear identity—and to show that soccer in the US had moved forward. We'd established all those goals already, but we wanted more. We wanted more because we knew we were good enough to earn more, but at the same time, we wanted to keep expectations in check.

I had some fun with reporters, asking my own question—"Has the US arrived?"—and then emphatically answering it: "Not even close. We're not pretending to be at the same level as the established teams, but the gap has closed considerably." Then I added, looking ahead to Germany, "On paper, it looks to be no match. However, we don't play this game on paper."

Before the game, I told the players: "Don't give them any respect. We should be in the semifinals."

That was a great game. I've always said that we have to be ourselves and play to our strengths. We're never going to be the most talented team, but we can be one of the toughest to beat, one of the fittest and most competitive, one of the most motivated. For us to win, we have to play our way, no one else's way, and we did that against Germany. To a lot of people, including the German soccer legend Franz Beckenbauer, known in Germany as Der Kaiser, we outplayed the Germans and deserved to win. We had our chances, that's for sure. The Germans scored one goal on a free kick and header from midfielder Michael Ballack, and then goalkeeper Oliver Kahn made that one goal stand up. He made great save after great save. And there was a call that could have gone our way, a hand ball at the goal line that wasn't called a penalty kick. To this day, I still cannot believe we weren't awarded a penalty kick there, but a team like Germany often gets a call here and there, given their years of competitiveness. We could have done more with our chances, but we didn't. We had to accept our fate and walk off the field, taking satisfaction in having gone toe-to-toe with Germany and having held our own.

"You showed the world you can play," I told the guys afterward.

"I thought we played them off the park, to be honest," DaMarcus Beasley says now. "After the Mexico game, we were on a high. We didn't have any fear. We had full confidence in everybody. We played our best game that day, one hundred percent. Better than the Portugal game. Better than the Mexico game. Against Germany was the best game that I had been a part of with that team, and I didn't even play. I was on the bench. But I know. You felt it in the stadium. It was a great moment, but we didn't get through."

Four years earlier, the Germans had embarrassed us. This time, we could hold our heads high. In our bus ride back to the hotel afterward, someone discovered a karaoke machine, and after the kind of singing that sets the dogs howling, someone put on Frank Sinatra singing "My Way," and guys started singing.

"Pretty much the whole team joined in," DeMarcus remembers. "At the end of the day we were a team, so we won as a team and we lost as a team."

The spirit I felt in that bus was amazing. The sense of camaraderie, of being in it together, was so electric, you felt the hairs on the back of your neck standing up. I was proud of my coaching staff and proud of my players. We'd given it our all. We'd showed we could do it our way and make it count. There would be time to kick ourselves, realizing that you never know when you'll get another shot, but riding in that bus we were spent and we were satisfied and we had no regrets.

Germany

We knew we had moved US soccer forward with our showing in South Korea and Japan, the best for the United States at the World Cup in seventy-two years, but when it came to developing the sport in this country, it always felt like one step forward, two steps back, one step forward, two steps back. I remember sitting at home in February 2005 and watching an NBA game, I think it was San Antonio against Miami, and the announcer, Brent Musburger, started talking about the increasing number of high-profile international players who had joined the NBA. Fine, fair point. True enough. Then he went on to say—and I still can't believe this—that David Stern had made basketball the number-one sport in the world. Are you kidding me? It was so embarrassing, like watching a grade school kid in short pants telling a classroom that his one-eyed mutt's the bestest dog in the world. Basketball and baseball combined can't touch soccer's international profile. They are regional diversions compared to the world sport.

In the aftermath of the 2002 World Cup, I wasn't sure what my future held. My agent, Richard Motzkin, had received calls from teams in the English Premier League asking about my availability, and that was a challenge I might have enjoyed taking on. I loved coaching the US national team, but I wasn't taking anything for granted. We worked out a new contract, and that August the new FIFA international rankings were announced, and the US team had cracked the top ten for the first time ever.

I did run into some trouble in 2004. Say this about me: I'm honest. My mouth might get me into trouble sometimes, but I prefer to be direct and to the point. It's just who I am. I love listening to Howard Stern. He's actually a Long Island guy like me. He says what's on his mind, nothing sugar-coated about it. That's how I was in those years, but I've mellowed a little over time. Maybe that's why I have no interest in going on Twitter and telling people what I'm thinking at a given moment. Nobody needs to hear my opinions when I'm sitting in my living room shouting at the TV.

In September 2004, I did an interview with Jack Bell of the *New York Times* and talked the way I always do, bluntly and honestly. There were some consequences. Jack's article was headlined "The US Coach Sounds Off," and that was pretty much what I did. I blasted some of the weird decisions being made by US Soccer and Major League Soccer.

"For the league to play games during World Cup qualifying is insane," I told Bell. "It shows a lack of respect for the national team. Ideally, the league should synchronize its schedule with the rest of the world. . . . People are pulling in opposite directions. Every coach, and I can't blame them, is trying to be successful. And they will call me, every coach. The decision to play games during qualifying is their problem."

I was just saying aloud what everyone knew. As the article mentioned, a majority of leagues around the world suspended play for qualifying games.

Jack did get me talking, and once I start, sometimes I say more than I need to say. For example, I also mentioned the fact that most MLS games "mean nothing," and shared my conviction that "in soccer, we don't have any administrators with soccer skills, in terms of knowing the game, and that is the case at US Soccer and MLS." It was a true statement, but it didn't go over very well.

MLS Commissioner Don Garber was so pissed off, he tried hard to get rid of me. If you ask me, my job was never in danger, but Grant Wahl later wrote in *Sports Illustrated* that the controversy over that *Times* article left me "close to being fired." Garber shot off an angry letter to Bob Contiguglia, president of US Soccer at the time, and they had me come in to talk to them and sit through a thorough airing of their concerns.

"There was a lot of pressure from MLS owners to do something, but we didn't," Bob told Grant Wahl. "I stood in the way."

Bob was on his way out as president of US Soccer, and Sunil Gulati would be taking over in 2006. I'd known Sunil for years, going back to the days when he was a water boy and I was coaching in the Olympic development program. That same year, 2004, my father died of lung cancer, and it always meant a lot to me that Sunil came to my father's funeral. My dad had a rough time late in life. He really missed my mother, who had passed away back in 1990. He tried living with my brother out in Phoenix, but then came back to New York. Sunil was there at the wake along with Chuck Blazer, who in those years was on FIFA's executive committee (and lived in Trump Tower with two rooms, one just for his cats—but that's another story).

Our top-ten FIFA ranking coming out of the last World Cup cycle gave us a boost, and by 2006 that ranking had improved to fifth in the world, but we knew none of it meant anything if we couldn't continue to move US soccer forward. Our path to the 2006 World Cup in Germany was not as eventful as four years earlier. By June 2005, when we traveled to Panama for a qualifying game and won 3–0, we knew we'd basically secured our spot. We clinched outright that September with a 2–0 win over Mexico in Columbus, Ohio, our seventh victory over the Mexicans in our last ten meetings.

I've said it before and I'll say it again: your chances in the World Cup rise and fall with your luck in the draw, and that December we all had to digest a tough one for us. We'd have to contend with the Czech Republic, Italy, and Ghana, a very challenging trio of teams, if we were going to get out of group play and try to improve on our 2002 showing.

Landon Donovan and DaMarcus Beasley had helped spark our breakthrough performance in South Korea, and we were looking to develop more young talent. Just as I'd brought Landon and DaMarcus along slowly, bringing them into camp to get a feel for what would be expected of them in the future, in May 2006 I had the pleasure of bringing Michael Bradley to his first training camp with the US national team. I'd held Michael as a baby and been close to him and his family for years. Michael earned his first cap in a May 26 friendly against Venezuela. We knew he was a big part of our future, but his time had not come quite yet.

Our first game in Germany was a fiasco. We knew the Czechs would be tough, but we thought we'd match up well against them, our speed likely to assert itself against an aging Czech lineup. It didn't work out that way. We were thoroughly outplayed that day in Gelsenkirchen. The Czechs scored on a header in the fifth minute and cruised to an easy 3–0 win. It was easy because we made it easy for them.

"We definitely gave the game away," our keeper, Kasey Keller, said afterward.

"Four years of planning and expectation, and two years of qualifying, unraveled disastrously in five minutes for the United States at the World Cup today in a humiliating 3–0 defeat to the Czech Republic," Jere Longman wrote in the *New York Times*.

"As soccer's global championship entered its fourth day, the reeling Americans suffered the ignominy of the tournament's most lopsided loss so far."

I was beside myself at the lack of intensity our guys showed.

Landon Donovan, I said afterward, "showed no aggressiveness," and "we got nothing from" DaMarcus Beasley.

Landon didn't disagree with my comments. "Yeah, that's true," he said, calling the game "embarrassing" and saying the team was "a little bit lifeless, a little bit unlucky. . . . Not enough guys came to play; that's what mattered."

A lesson I'll always take away from that game is that you never want to hear your players talking about not knowing their roles. Team chemistry and team communication were always my focus, going back to my first days as a coach, and I'd always taken the view that you wanted your players as comfortable as possible with what you expected of them. There were a lot of ways that could go sideways, some partly your fault, some having nothing to do with you. When DaMarcus said after the Czech Republic game, "I don't know what he wants me to do!" that was ultimately on me, even if DaMarcus should have known just what I wanted him to do, whether he was being asked to play right back or jump into the attack. Other players talked about having the sense that not everyone knew their role. I knew I never wanted to go down that road again as US team coach, but the first order of business was to make some changes going into an Italy game that we had to win to have any shot at advancing.

I decided it was time to see what Clint Dempsey could do for us. Clint was a hard-nosed kid out of East Texas who always played with intensity, as if he had a chip on his shoulder. That stuff never bothered me. Everybody's different. That was a week after his twenty-first birthday, and I felt he was ready and gave him the news he'd be playing. "I remember it was tough to sleep the night before the game," Clint says now. "All I kept thinking about was taking advantage of the moment, making it happen, not looking back and having any regrets at all. When someone gives you such a big opportunity like that, you just want to go out there and make the most of it."

As a proud Italian American and the son of even prouder Italian Americans, the game obviously had special significance for me. I had my father's mass card in my pocket during the game. The game against Italy was going to be extremely challenging for our team. The Italians are known for their tough defending, physical qualities, and gamesmanship. They are historically strong in group play and know how to advance. They're proud and confident, and we went into the game reeling after our 3–0 loss to the Czech Republic but determined to make a better showing.

We met the challenge. Italy went ahead early, inspiring much talk about how against Italy, a 1–0 lead might as well 10–0 because the Italian defense is so solid, but then an own goal made it 1–1—and the game got uglier and uglier. Daniele De Rossi elbowed McBride in the cheek, drawing blood and earning a red card and ejection to drop the Italians down to ten men, but then our defender Pablo Mastroeni also earned a red card for a hard tackle. McBride came to the sideline and took three stitches, then didn't stop running all game long.

Early in the second half, Eddie Pope picked up his second yellow card and was sent off. That was three ejections in one game, only the fourth time that had happened in the World Cup up to then. We had to survive forty-three minutes with only nine players on the field to preserve the tie, and somehow we did it. Clint Dempsey, playing in his first World Cup, had a good game for us, generating scoring chances and playing with his usual fearlessness.

"I just wanted to run and play with no fear, and I felt like I was able to do that," Clint says now. "I felt the team played well. We almost could have won the game."

I brought DaMarcus Beasley on for Clint in the second half, and he used his speed, seeming to score a goal that was waved off on an offside call that made no sense to me. I was proud of my guys, the way they hung in there, even in such difficult circumstances, and gave their all. When it was finally over, the players collapsed to the field in exhaustion. I really don't think they had any more to give.

"Not many teams could hold their poise like that," I said afterward, head held high. "That's the kind of team the US should be putting out there."

"Out of humiliation came a desperate form of gallantry," *Times* columnist George Vecsey wrote. "Embarrassed by their last game, the United States held off Italy, 1–1, in a World Cup match of ejections and mistakes and ultimately of honor."

We weren't packing our bags just yet. Ghana had surprised the Czech Republic, 2–0, which meant that if we beat Ghana, we might still have a shot at moving out of our group. For that to happen, we knew, we'd have to get a few breaks—but we didn't. Ghana took a 1–0 lead and then we equalized late in the first half when Clint Dempsey scored off a DaMarcus Beasley cross. We felt we could pull the game out, but a questionable call led to a Ghana penalty kick, which they converted, and as hard as we worked to answer, we couldn't break through.

We weren't about to try to focus on positives at the time, but that World Cup launched Clint on his way to becoming the US men's team's leading all-time scorer, tied with Landon Donovan. "It was a dream come true to start in a World Cup, because I knew what it was like to be in the U20 World Cup and not really play," Clint remembers. "So there I was, thinking here's another World Cup where the game will go by and I won't really have an impact on it, and actually to end up being the only American to score a goal in that World Cup, and make an impact like that, was pretty special."

We were downcast and miserable heading home early, three and out. Looking back on it now, the important thing was to draw some lessons. We had work to do as a national program, that was clear, and in the years since then we have seen improvement in the level of play in Major League Soccer. We're developing US talent, but we have to do more with it. We need to produce not one Christian Pulisic, but many more.

What matters is results, specifically World Cup results. Going into Germany, we had a four-year cycle that was as successful as any ever for the US program. We won Gold Cups, we had a comfortable time qualifying for the World Cup, we climbed in the world rankings and went into Germany ranked fourth internationally, which may have been unrealistically high, but it showed that we'd come a long way as a program. Then we fell short. So much was right, even if it didn't look that way from the outside all the time, but we needed a little more.

There was a legendary college football coach, Darrell Royal, who led the Texas Longhorns to a 167-47-5 mark over twenty years starting in the late 1950s. He had a colorful way with a quote. One time he said, "You've got to think lucky. If you fall into a mudhole, check your back pocket. You might have caught a fish." It was Darrell Royal who said, after a tough loss in 1965, "There's an old saying, 'You dance with the one that brung ya.'" That might make sense in college football, but not—I realized after the Germany fiasco of 2006—in World Cup soccer.

Going into the games in Germany, the unfortunate fact was that some of the players who got us into the World Cup were perhaps by then a little too old for the international game and simply not good enough to make us better in 2006. Looking back, I probably should have made a couple of changes on that 2006 team to improve both our quality and enthusiasm as a team. We didn't quite have the leadership we needed, though we did have some exceptional leaders. Brian McBride was brilliant. With any team he was ever with, Brian always thought about the team first, and, believe me, I'm not that naive in thinking that Brian never thought about Brian, but he was as good a team player as I've ever seen. We needed more of those guys on that 2006 team.

Part III

Turnaround in LA

11

Back in MLS

B ack in the early days of MLS, starting with the first season in 1996, it was a crap shoot whether the league had any future or how it would evolve. No one knew what the hell was going on. They had a business plan that lasted about a week, and then they realized it wasn't going to happen the way they thought it was. The league had come a long way ten years later when I rejoined MLS in July 2006 as sporting director and coach of the New York Red Bulls, but I figured out pretty quickly that the job was not a good fit for me and I'd probably made a mistake taking it.

My first game coaching the Red Bulls, less than a month after US Soccer announced I was out as national team coach, was against Barcelona at Giants Stadium in front of a sellout crowd of 79,002, the second largest crowd to watch a soccer game at Giants Stadium. A young Argentine player by the name of Lionel Messi ran circles around us all day. Ronaldinho scored twice, and we lost 4–1. Our MLS record at that point stood at 3-6-8, good for last place in the Eastern Conference.

My time with the Red Bulls was a learning experience from beginning to end. I take full responsibility for making a questionable decision in taking the job. I did not understand well enough what I was getting into. I believed promises I should not have believed. "This is a challenging situation," I said at the press conference that July announcing me as the new coach. "This is a unique opportunity. We plan to build a first-class training facility for our whole organization from the senior team to the academy, and Red Bull has the resources to do that."

Emphasis on "plan." I waited and waited to see those plans move forward. Red Bull took control of the franchise in early 2006, but they were not properly advised and prepared by MLS on the challenges of ownership in the league. They simply were not prepared to run a team. We had no real practice facilities, for the New York Giants had control of the stadium field. Some days, we would drive around New Jersey looking for a grass field to train on. A video of us driving around in vain, which was what happened most times, would pretty well sum up the feeling around the team that year. We had no stadium, and planning for one was extremely challenging. The roster I inherited from Alexi Lalas was weak and required a lot of work. There was no consensus within the organization as to how the roster could be improved. Last and maybe worst of all, the company wanted to run the club from its international headquarters in Salzburg, Austria, which created obvious difficulties. That's a long ways away. The club was a mess, and taking that position was a dumb move on my part. To this day, this franchise has yet to win the MLS Cup in its twenty-two years of existence. However, they have become a much-improved franchise, and I do think their day will come.

My hope for my first season with the Red Bulls was to make the playoffs, but that was no small challenge, since we were in last place when I started. We did that, and basically played even with DC United that October in our two-game playoff, but narrowly fell short and watched them advance. I guess DC United liked what they saw of me on the sideline during that playoff series. One of the owners of the team, Will Chang, called me after the season and said he wanted to meet with me to see if I might come back to coach DC United again. Will was in Toronto and said he'd try to come see me in Charlottesville, but he needed an international airport, so I agreed to drive to Richmond, an hour and a half away, and meet him for lunch. We had a great talk, but I wasn't ready to jump.

"I really have a commitment to Red Bull," I told him at lunch. "The Red Bulls told me they would build new practice facilities for us and a new stadium."

So I opted not to make the move, figuring it was worth seeing how things would develop with the new facilities. The managing director called me in the off-season to tell me how well it was all going.

"As we talk, we're building the field," he told me.

I went back to New Jersey in January and found out they hadn't done anything. I learned a number of lessons from my Red Bulls experience. One, I didn't do my homework properly. If you do your homework, it's a lot harder to be sold a bill of goods, the way I was. I was promised the support to take us to the MLS Cup, but it never came through. We did qualify for the playoffs in both my years, 2006 and 2007, but I was out of a job one day after we lost to New England in the MLS playoffs in November 2007. I came into the office the next day and met with the team's managing director, Marc de Grandpre.

"We're firing you," he said.

"I have a contract," I said.

I told him he could talk to my agent, Richard Motzkin, about the year remaining on my contract at $1.25 million, and I got out of there. The truth was, I was mostly happy. Given everything, my 16-16-10 record with the Red Bulls counted as a triumph. I knew the Red Bulls were nowhere near being ready to compete, and I'd had enough of being misled. I left the office and drove straight to Charlottesville and never looked back.

I figured taking it easy for a while wouldn't be a bad thing.

John Skipper, president of ESPN, asked me if I'd like to work as a soccer commentator, and I drove up to RFK Stadium for the 2007 MLS Cup to talk it over in person with John. We'd all but worked out the deal when MLS Commissioner Don Garber, no fan of my outspoken approach, did his best to block ESPN from hiring me. I don't know what Don was so afraid of.

I'd always been interested in teaching and had a chance to do more of that. I had a friend in the school of education at the University of Virginia, and I agreed to teach a graduate course on leadership in athletics. I was excited about it, and put in a lot of time to get the syllabus approved. When I got a call from Tim Leiweke of the LA Galaxy, asking me to fly out to Los Angeles in August 2008 to talk about possibly coaching again, my first thought was that the plane ride would give me some good work time to go over my curriculum. I could also come up with lesson plans for the first couple weeks. That was just what I did on that flight, too.

The class was going to focus on leadership in athletics, highlighting the Duke lacrosse scandal, which demonstrated the breakdown of leadership at the university. Three Duke lacrosse players were indicted on a false rape charge by a student at another local university, and the whole lacrosse team was punished. Those cases have to be taken very seriously and handled carefully. In that case, however, the initial investigation was a farce. The charges were later dropped, the prosecutor in the case was disbarred for withholding evidence, and the *Raleigh News and Observer* columnist who had whipped people up against the lacrosse team apologized in print. That was going to be an interesting class, going through it all again, trying to learn from it.

I'd been enjoying myself, getting a little break from being in the thick of the action, but I'm not going to lie: California had a lot to offer. For one, I loved the idea of a team just going for it in every way, which was what the Galaxy had been doing. Led by Tim, CEO of the Anschutz Entertainment Group, which also owned the LA Kings and a minority interest in the LA Lakers, the Galaxy had made a giant splash in January 2007 by signing David Beckham, the most visible soccer player on the planet, after having already landed Landon Donovan, the most visible US soccer player, two years earlier. They hadn't been winning, but they were a hungry franchise.

I joined Tim and Dan Beckerman in a private area of the Stadium Club, and before the game even started, we'd had a couple of nice bottles of wine along with dinner. Tim had come to make a deal.

"I think we shocked him because we made the deal on the spot," Tim remembers.

It takes a lot to shock me, but I was agreeably surprised. Then again, I was also surprised that Tim offered me a one-year contract.

"Why would I do that?" I asked him.

No sane coach ever wants to work on a one-year contract. Talk about having the deck stacked against you.

"Listen, just talk to my agent, Motzkin," I told him.

One of my demands was that they also hire my longtime assistant, Dave Sarachan, a head coach in his own right, who was MLS Coach of the Year in 2003 for the Chicago Fire. I wanted Dave at my side. Tim took it in stride. He turned to Dan Beckerman, also at the dinner.

"All right, you're going to have to go negotiate a deal with Dave," he said. "Good luck!"

So as we sat in Tim's box watching the game, Tim and Richard were talking on the phone. By halftime they had a deal done for a three-year contract. I had my concerns, but after the disaster at New York Red Bull, the Galaxy had what I wanted: a quality stadium and training facilities, great weather, and local management with a great attitude. With Red Bull I'd had no support from ownership and no direction from anybody. Having to sit around and wait for an answer to come back from Austria just wasn't my style. That was not going to be an issue this time around. I drove home that night thinking, *Listen, at the very least, I've got Landon Donovan and David Beckham. That's a pretty good start.*

I knew that Tim Leiweke and the organization believed in me and what I could do, and that made all the difference. Maybe it's good I didn't know that night over dinner and wine just how high they were on me. "We weren't letting Bruce out without getting a deal done," Tim says now. "We had a very long conversation about our ambition as a league and a club. What I liked about Bruce is that he wasn't afraid of that ambition. A lot of people would be afraid of the pressure of grand ambitions like putting the league on our shoulders. Many people don't aspire to change a sport, a league, in one fell swoop. I think Bruce loved that. He loved the stage. He loved the commitment that AEG and Mr. Anschutz were willing to make. He aspired, as we did, to seize the moment to redefine our league and our team."

They'd gone with Ruud Gullit as coach as part of a larger effort to build an international profile for the Galaxy and in turn Major League Soccer. I'm not saying the idea didn't make sense. Maybe they had to try that. But coaching an MLS team is different than coaching in Europe, and not necessarily easier.

Tim now says:

From the first day we were involved in Major League Soccer, we always thought about hiring Bruce. What was unique and relevant with the Galaxy, we felt the pressure of trying to build a brand that from an international standpoint would bring new credibility to the league and new upside to where we could all go. Were we building a super club? I don't think we thought in those terms, but we did feel we had to lead the league and assume the mantle of being the model franchise. So we went out and got David, spent a lot of money, we got Landon back from Europe. We experimented on an international coach, who gave us that kind of international branding, but he didn't understand Major League Soccer. We needed the greatest coach ever. That was always our vision. We had to make sure the timing was right. Bruce is in my opinion the best coach in the history of Major League Soccer. His track record and accomplishments speak for themselves.

LA

For years I'd been kidding all the California guys I coached on the national team. I'd ride them all the time for being soft. Then I moved out to California to take over the Galaxy, and I finally understood. California was a whole different world, and I loved it. Phyllis and I bought a place in Manhattan Beach, and she drove cross-country to bring our golden retriever out, because we wouldn't put him on a plane. My first two were Joshua and Toby, and the third one I named T.J., partly for Thomas Jefferson, whose Monticello plantation was near Charlottesville. T.J. was the greatest dog, and Manhattan Beach was a good place for him. It was 70 degrees every day with the ocean a few blocks away, and I was neighbors with people I enjoyed talking to about sports, like Don Mattingly, manager of the Los Angeles Dodgers at the time, and Steve Nash, the former NBA point guard who was part of a regular soccer game near where we lived in Manhattan Beach. What was not to like?

I knew I had a big job on my hands with the Galaxy as both general manager and head coach. The club was 6-8-6 and winless in its last eight games when I took over. For my first game as coach, we were without our best players, Beckham, Donovan, and striker Carlos Ruiz, because all three were with their national teams for games that week, and actually Ruiz never rejoined the team. The Galaxy had missed the playoffs the year before and looked in danger of missing again.

"There's no way we're making the playoffs with this team," I told Tim Leiweke that first week.

That didn't mean I wasn't going to give it a try. My first win after taking over the Galaxy came on September 20 against DC United, my former team. Landon had a hat trick and an assist, and we won 5–2. That was enough to spark some optimism about turning it around, but we won only one more game the rest of the season and the Galaxy missed the playoffs for the third season in a row. Landon led the MLS in scoring with twenty goals and was named MVP of the Galaxy, but he was frustrated at going through another difficult season.

Taking over a team on the fly, starting in midseason, you're limited in how much impact you can have. Mostly I was watching and learning, getting a feel for what we would need to do to turn the Galaxy around fast. Once we were eliminated, we could turn to the work of the off-season, which was rebuilding in as literal a sense as you ever see in sports. Other than Landon and David, no one was in a secure position, and we went looking for as many good players as we could find to upgrade position by position but, more important, put together a group that played together as a team. I'd say that out of a roster of twenty-four players that first off-season, we kept only five or six.

In those days you had a little bit more flexibility in bringing in players to your MLS club, so I brought in players I knew previously, like Gregg Berhalter, Jovan Kirovski, Tony Sanneh, and Eddie Lewis, who had all played for me on the national team. We took a trip down to Brazil to scout players and took a flyer on four young Brazilians whom I brought in with us for a monthlong

trial, and amazingly enough, two of the four stuck, Juninho (Vi-
tor Gomes Pereira Júnior) and Leonardo (José Leonardo Ribeiro
da Silva). We developed them into players we could use with the
Galaxy by the 2010 season, and through the end of the 2017 season, they were still both playing in Major League Soccer.

We were lucky in the draft, which as most people understood
is always a bit of a crapshoot. A lot of this stuff is pretty basic.
If you're looking for good college players, what do you do? We
needed help at the defensive end and found two players who'd just
won the College Cup championship with the University of Maryland in College Park. With our first-round pick (third overall), we
went for a Dallas-born defender named Omar Gonzalez who at
six-five would stand out in a crowd. A. J. DeLaGarza, another
defender out of Maryland, was our second-round pick.

At the Galaxy you always knew you had people behind you
who were in it to win it. I'd met the owner, Philip Anschutz, in
1998 when I was coaching DC United. Phil was an interesting figure. He'd grown up in Kansas, son of an oil tycoon and neighbor
to the future US senator Bob Dole, and had made a lot of smart
investments over the years to become one of the wealthiest people
in the country. When I met Phil, he had recently come back from
the 1998 World Cup in France, and he was excited to help grow
soccer in the United States. He was a cofounder of MLS and at
one point owned six different franchises, though he was losing
money. I remember that Phil in the early going said, "If I own an
NFL team, I'm just going to be another rich guy in the room. In
soccer I can make a difference."

Phil worked with Tim Leiweke, who was P. T. Barnum in the
best sense, a born promoter overflowing with energy and interest
in everything all at once. "I'm more emotional," Tim says. "I get
pumped up. Bruce is equally passionate. You just don't see it on
the surface." As the *New Yorker* put it in a 2012 Connie Bruck
profile, Tim is "an inspired salesman, not given to modesty or

understatement." The two met in the 1990s in Leiweke's days as president of the Denver Nuggets basketball team, which needed land to build what became the Pepsi Center and bought a parcel from Anschutz, one of the largest landholders in the world. So in 1996 when Phil decided to send someone out to take over the Los Angeles Kings of the NHL and build a complex like the Pepsi Center, he figured Tim was his guy.

"When Anschutz's multiple entities were rolled into Anschutz Entertainment Group, in 1999, he put Tim Leiweke in charge of the global brand," Bruck reported. "Today, A.E.G. owns or operates about a hundred venues around the world, including the O2 arenas in London, Berlin, and Hamburg, and controls much of their content. Anschutz and Leiweke have transformed the sports and entertainment industry."

Tim's energy made all the difference with AEG. He took the idea and ran with it, and built a multi-billion-dollar company from the ground up. No one really knew where it was going, but Tim did. Phil is a man who avoids the limelight, and especially the media. As that *New Yorker* article put it, on visits to LA, and presumably everywhere else, "he is accompanied by no chauffeur, personal assistant, or bodyguard. He does not use a cell phone, or e-mail."

You would never think Phil would be involved in live entertainment and all that stuff, but Tim had a vision. From what he told me, you don't make much on the concerts, but if you own the building, you make your money through sponsorships and marketing. I went to see the Rolling Stones at the Staples Center with Dan Beckerman, who ended up taking over for Tim as CEO of AEG in 2013, and he told me the concert costs them maybe $5.1 million and they expected to gross about $5.2 million. Tim found a way to make it work. The only businesses they didn't make any money off of were the Kings and the Galaxy, although the franchise values soared.

Tim had been the one to fly all over the world to talk to David Beckham about what it could mean playing in Los Angeles. Alexi Lalas was general manager of the Galaxy at the time, but it was Tim who got David excited about the possibilities. As Tim remembers now, "I met with David probably half a dozen times. We met once when he was in LA, we went over and met with him in London, we went over and met with him in Spain. There were a variety of meetings to continue to convince him this was an opportunity to remake a sport."

David, always intrigued about a fresh challenge, liked what he heard. "Tim's passion, and his energy, and his love for the Galaxy, and his love for the game plus Major League Soccer, excited me, and that kind of made my mind up," David says now.

You could study Beckham's time in LA as a classic example of the rewards and risks of building a team around major stars, but especially the rewards. *Sports Illustrated* soccer writer Grant Wahl wrote a book called *The Beckham Experiment*, but that book came out early in David's time in LA, so it was a little like a newspaper sportswriter publishing a game story at halftime. My own take on David, going way back, was always that he was a self-aware young man who was very competitive and very serious about everything to do with playing the sport he loved. By the time he signed with the Galaxy, he was the most famous footballer on the planet, and everyone always wanted to talk about his wife, the former Victoria Adams, Posh Spice of the pop group the Spice Girls, and their children. But really, when you're training or getting ready for a game or trying to get the equalizer three minutes into stoppage time, that stuff's all totally irrelevant and off your radar.

It's true: you never want one player to be bigger than the team or to think that he or she is bigger than the team. Kobe Bryant was a great basketball player, but there were times when the Lakers were Kobe and a bunch of guys who weren't Kobe, wondering what Kobe wanted that day. Another thing to remember about elite athletes is that if they're going to be difficult, they tend to do so at the end of their careers when they can't get it done on the field or on the court anymore, but they still have the same mentality and they still want to be treated the same. That's a delicate proposition, getting the most out of players in that phase of their careers, and it requires a skill set all its own.

I think I was lucky in a lot of ways. I worked with David Beckham and Landon Donovan (and later Robbie Keane), who were all dealing with late-career transitions at one time or another, and mostly I had amazingly positive experiences with them. I have to give Tim Leiweke credit for having the vision and the passion to bring David to North America. I don't think in retrospect anyone can question that it was a great move that was huge for the development of soccer in this country, and Tim made it happen.

"Tim Leiweke and Alexi Lalas flew over to Madrid to talk to me about joining LA Galaxy and Major League Soccer, and that was long enough ago that the league was nowhere near as developed as it now is," David remembers. "I had doubts, but I was curious—and I was open. Tim made a very persuasive case. He had me excited about the possibilities. I'd played my entire career in Europe up until then and I was going to do something that had totally not been done before."

I had the sense that David was having doubts about his choice to come play in North America when I first joined the Galaxy as coach. Who could blame him? Six months had elapsed from the time he signed the contract to join Galaxy and until he'd actually arrived, and in the interim he'd played his way back into the Real Madrid lineup. Then he came over to California and had a disappointing first season with the Galaxy because of injuries. Because David was always looking to play in another World Cup for England and needed playing time in Europe to stay sharp, the injuries were all the more frustrating for him.

The same month I got the Galaxy job, in August 2008, David was featured as a star of the closing ceremonies of the Summer Olympics in Beijing, which had an international audience of more than two billion people. For the handover ceremony to the Olympics four years later in London, a double-decker bus entered the stadium and turned into a stage—for musicians, including Jimmy Page of Led Zeppelin, and for David Beckham, taking a soccer ball from a Chinese girl as a symbolic handoff. That's how big David was, as if any of us ever forgot it.

The sense I had from David when I first took the Galaxy job was that he was looking at other options. Beckham at the time was away on international duty for the English national team; I called him, and he did not sound happy. When David came back to Southern California, we met at his house in Beverly Hills. I remember that his wife, Victoria, answered the door. We had a glass of wine and talked, but the whole time I'm wondering, *What in the hell is this guy thinking?* He was playing with Real Madrid, made the jump to MLS only to find himself playing for a team with some major issues. The Galaxy finished in fifth place in the Western Conference in 2007, his first season, with a 9-14-7 record. Our final mark for 2008 would be 8-13-9.

"I know you're looking around and maybe you're questioning 'What did I do?'" I said to David. "All I can tell you is I'm going to do my best to rebuild the team."

He liked my determination. I asked for his support, and he said I had it all the way. We talked about some potential problem areas, including his relationship with Landon Donovan. I made the point that he and Landon didn't have to hang out away from the team, but they did need to have a good working relationship. That was all that mattered. I knew David had to make the choice that was right for him—and his family.

We loaned him to AC Milan in the off-season for three months starting January 2009, which was a good way for David to stay sharp, and he found himself loving life in Italy. Why not? I enjoy hanging out in Italy as well. Who doesn't? He started talking about wanting to stay longer. "I have expressed my desire to stay at AC Milan now, and it's just down to Milan and Galaxy to come to an agreement," David said from Milan in early February. "I have enjoyed my time here. I knew I would enjoy it but I didn't expect to enjoy it as much as I have and do as well as I have." As a *New York Times* headline put it in February 2009, "Beckham Hopes to Revel in the Joys of Milan in the Spring."

Look, it wasn't ideal, but from my perspective it was all fine. Playing with Milan was good for David, and, provided we got him back early enough in the season for our purposes, that was good for us as well. The deal we came up with actually called for David to pitch in some of his own money to stay a little longer with Milan, which showed how important it was to him, given how focused he was on making the England World Cup team in 2010. None of it ever interfered with David's value as a spokesman for the game in this country. In fact, that March he did interviews with ESPN and with Matt Lauer on the *Today* show to emphasize that he was committed to Major League Soccer and the Galaxy.

I never worried about David. My position has always been I don't much care what you do when you're away from the team, so long as you show up on time, ready to train hard or play hard, and fully prepared and fully focused. David Beckham to me is a real winner. He's always determined. Regardless of his reputation and multiple other interests in fashion and so on, David was all business when he stepped onto the field, in training and in games. I have the greatest respect for him. I knew he'd be ready to play when he came back from Italy, and that was all that mattered to me.

David and Landon

It wasn't complicated. Maybe that's the main lesson of dealing with these potentially difficult situations: *Don't make them more complicated than they need to be*—not in how you think of them, not in how you talk about them, and not how you deal with them. I knew David and Landon were both professionals who wanted the same things, and I knew their styles of play and strengths on the field well enough to know they could have great chemistry as teammates. They just needed to get through a transition period that in their case had been complicated by the team going through a tough season or two. I didn't want any drama. I just wanted to move past anything that needed moving past, so I called Landon and David into my Galaxy office for a quick face-to-face meeting to clear the air.

There had been talk of some issues between David and Landon, most of which I tuned out. There's always a lot of chatter out there, and most of it amounts to nothing. Landon talked to Grant Wahl at a time when he was clearly frustrated from a long, difficult 2008 season, and he did a little venting. He's human.

Then Wahl and *Sports Illustrated* took more of an *Us Weekly* approach as opposed to the more literate *SI* tradition started by great writers like Frank Deford and Ron Fimrite. The July 6, 2009, issue of the magazine carried an excerpt from Wahl's book under the headline "How Beckham Blew It" with a blurb that threw around words like *failed* and *alienated*. I didn't take any of it very seriously. When you're on the inside looking out, you just chuckle at that kind of stuff and move on.

Who really cares about stories of players going out for a meal together on the road, and Beckham being told he couldn't drink unless he showed ID? I guess they call that human interest. The parts that had people talking were the quotations, some of them a little surprising. I'm not going to rehash all of them here. It was the same kind of stuff teammates often say about each other when they're going through a stretch of losing and things aren't working. Great players hate losing as much as everyone else, probably a lot more, and frustrations build. Landon was quoted questioning whether David was giving his all for the team, and saying things like "All that we care about at a minimum is that he committed himself to us. As time has gone on, that has not proven to be the case in many ways—on the field, off the field."

David and Landon were going to be fine. I never had any doubt about that, but one thing a life in coaching had taught me is that you always grab the bull by the horns and go straight at a potential problem. Soon before David made his 2009 debut with the team that July, I told David and Landon I wanted them to come into my office the next morning for a meeting.

"Listen, the only way this team has a chance of getting good is if the three of us can work together," I said in a no-nonsense but friendly tone.

David and Landon were both with me. There was no resistance.

Landon admitted that he'd gone about things the wrong way

in sharing his frustration with a reporter. "I want to apologize," he told us. "I stand by the things I said, but I should have been a man and come and said it to you in person. That was a learning experience to me."

David didn't say much. Mostly he listened. But I remember he was big enough to say, "Listen, I can put aside any of these issues. Landon is my teammate. We're going to do everything we can to be a good team."

This was maybe a ten-minute meeting.

"We walked in and quickly put it to bed," Landon remembers. "We said what we needed to say. I think that one meeting meant as much to the success of the Galaxy as anything that happened. It met it head on. Bruce made sure we were past it, so we were all on the same page and we could get on to trying to be successful to win."

It's the kind of thing that comes up all the time on teams, and as the coach you look for ways to go right after the problem or potential problem. Landon and David were both total professionals.

"There was just a lot of misunderstanding at the time," David says now. "We weren't that successful on the pitch at that time. People start to pick at things and ask questions like *Is there a problem between me and Landon?* I never had a problem with Landon. I loved him as a player, I liked him as a person."

That squares with everything I saw, and I was around these guys for years.

"We went out to dinners and socialized on the road," David says now. "When there was a book written and some things said about myself at the time, of course it wasn't nice. But at the end of the day, I'm a grown man. I've had a lot worse things said about me over my career. I can handle it. It didn't affect me on the field or off the field. I was more worried about how it might affect the team. Eventually it didn't become a problem, because

Bruce had this way about him that he handled it perfectly. We all wanted the same thing. We got on with it. Literally we sat down, Bruce said what he had to say, Landon said what he had to say, I listened and we got out of there. And got on with it on the pitch."

Landon puts it almost exactly the same way.

"We were all on the same page after that," Landon says now. "We felt the same way about it. We hadn't actually talked about it and addressed the book until then, at least not David and I. This was very fresh then. Having a chance to just get it over with was really important. It relieved a lot of stress for the both of us and allowed us to be focused on what we should be focused on, which was playing soccer."

That year we nearly won our first MLS Cup together, and probably should have, and obviously Beckham and Donovan were a big part of it. They were not the best of friends, and didn't need to be, but the fact we aired our dirty laundry, not in public but in private together as men, helped us get going in the right direction. We went into the room and discussed it and then any issues that we had along the way after that were always discussed the same way.

Landon, to his credit, learned from the experience. Players, like people in general, have different ways of handling loss, and sometimes we learn that what we thought we saw wasn't necessarily what we did see. "There were things I wasn't happy about with David, but none of them had to do with who he is as a person," Landon says now. "When I look at it retrospectively, David got himself in a position that was really difficult, and a lot of us would have reacted the same way. Then everything shifted and we were winning and everyone was happy."

David's first game for the Galaxy in the 2009 season was at Giants Stadium against my former team, the New York Red Bulls. The Grant Wahl stuff was still recent then, so David fielded questions at a press conference before the game, and it was a lively session.

Here's how William C. Rhoden of the *New York Times* described the scene:

"Grant Wahl, a writer for *Sports Illustrated* whose book *The Beckham Experiment* was published this week, asked Beckham how he justified being committed to the Galaxy and to M.L.S. when he is a part-time player this year and whether he will be a part-time player next year as well."

David stayed calm, but he answered the question in the spirit in which it was raised.

"Let me just clear this up first," David said. "Is this question for the second unofficial book or your magazine?"

We won that day in Giants Stadium, and soon the team was clicking more and more. We qualified for the playoffs for the first time in three years and made it all the way to the MLS Cup Final against Real Salt Lake. David and Landon set up Mike Magee for a goal that gave us a 1–0 lead, but they equalized, and the game—and that year's MLS season—came down to penalty kicks. David was dealing with a foot injury and had had some injections, but by this time they'd worn off, and he was wincing and noticeably limping when he stepped up for our first PK. He drilled his shot into the lower left corner. That got us off to a good start, but ultimately Nick Rimando, the Salt Lake keeper, had the best day, and they won on kicks. We were disappointed, but we knew we'd be back.

"Our players, our team, our organization had a great year," I said afterward. "Can't be disappointed. I think we did a great job in turning our team around."

Landon played that MLS off-season with Everton in the English Premier League, Tim Howard's team at the time, and gave them a shot in the arm. He was named the player of the month for January, an honor voted on by fans. David went on loan to

AC Milan again the next off-season, then tore his Achilles tendon in March, the kind of injury that can end a career, but he made a quick and complete recovery and rejoined our lineup by mid-September. Landon, our captain and leading goal scorer, led us to a 17-7-8 record that year, and we made it to the Western Conference finals, which we hosted before a sold-out crowd of twenty-seven thousand at the Home Depot Center. The year before in the MLS Cup, we probably should have won. Not this time. Dallas smoked us 3–0 to advance to the MLS Cup. We'd have to wait one more year.

I knew I was not going to have any problems with David Beckham, but working with him day in and day out, I was surprised at just how much I enjoyed being around his professionalism and passion for the game. He had a lot going on in his life, and I could understand how outsiders could come up with the idea that he was at times distracted from soccer, but that was not my experience of the man at all. He liked to joke around and enjoy his downtime, but when it was time to practice or play, he was always intensely focused. He and I had an understanding from the beginning, which only deepened with time. But let's give him a chance to check in with his own thoughts on working with me, from a conversation for the book:

> *Bruce has always been a fair manager. If he feels he should leave you out for a game, then he tells you; he doesn't just do it. That's one of those things Sir Alex Ferguson was always good at, I remember from my years at Manchester United; he would always tell you. I'm sure Bruce has been angry with me, and vice versa, but at the end of the day we're grown men. We put that aside and work together— and then we forget it.*
>
> *All great players need a ruthless streak that runs through their veins, and all great managers need that, and that's*

what Bruce has as well. Like a Sir Alex or a Carlo Ancelotti or a Sven-Göran Eriksson or a José Mourinho, Bruce is one of those coaches who always has respect for the players. Of course they're going to fall out with certain players at some points over the years; that's just natural. But whatever they do, you know the respect is there.

Bruce might pace around in the locker room a little bit before a big game, which might be a sign of nerves, but he has a calmness around him and the staff that I think helps relax the players before big games. He has a very dry sense of humor. I didn't get most of what he said. He's very sarcastic with things he says. Some people can't take that, but I enjoyed being around his sarcasm and dry jokes. He'd give just as good as he got. It was a challenge to keep up with him sometimes, and I liked that challenge. Bruce set me at ease right away when we first started working together with LA Galaxy.

A lot of people thought I was taking a big chance coming to America late in my career. They were right. I was. That was just what I wanted: a challenge. I knew what it had done for ice hockey when Wayne Gretzky left Edmonton in 1988 and signed with the Los Angeles Kings, becoming one of the greatest ambassadors for that sport in the US ever. I hoped to be an ambassador for soccer in a way that could get more people excited. That—and winning—were the challenges that brought me over.

I was playing for Real Madrid when the idea of trying to make a splash for the sport in California first started to take shape for me. I was Real Madrid Player of the Year for 2005–2006, but was told I'd be leaving the club at the end of the 2006–2007 season. I had opportunities with AC Milan and in Germany to consider. At thirty-two, I felt I could have played four more seasons at the top level in Europe if

I chose to stay. But being the kind of person I am, and the player I am, I always look for a bigger challenge.

I was always more aware of North American football than a lot of European players. I've always been a big soccer fan as well as a player, and always followed leagues around the world. I can never sleep after a game, so often I would be up late watching a game from New York or San Jose. I'd heard about Bruce Arena for quite a few years, and watched his teams play.

My first year and a half with the Galaxy were not easy. I came over and I had quite a bad injury when I first came, so I wasn't fit. I wasn't playing, and there was an unsettled feeling through the club. We weren't playing that well. We finished the 2007 season 9-14-7, fifth out of six teams in the Western Conference, and did not qualify for the playoffs. I saw only limited playing time. Late that year the team decided to buy out the contract of the coach, Frank Yallop, and replace him with Ruud Gullit, which I supported. I thought Ruud would work out well, but for whatever reason there were some frictions with some players, and a change was needed. I was in England, training with the national team, when I got a call from Bruce in August 2006 to tell me he was being named Galaxy coach.

It was an honest discussion. Up to that point I really had not established myself with the Galaxy. I set high standards for myself and had not reached them yet. So when I spoke to Bruce, a certain part of me was nervous. I'd never done a move like this before. I wasn't having second thoughts or anything, it was just a case of nerves. When Bruce came on the phone and we spoke and I heard it from the horse's mouth and knew he was coming to the Galaxy, that was the turning point for me. That was the turning point for me that made the Galaxy a better franchise. He made the team a lot better. There was a lot more settled atmosphere, a lot more professional atmosphere. I worked with Bruce to try to get more professionalism running throughout the team. That was the turning point for me, that was when I started really enjoying playing for the club.

Robbie Keane

Going into 2011, we felt strongly that we were one or two moves away from winning an MLS Cup. We were enjoying ourselves and loving the buzz the team was generating in Southern California. Life was good, and it was good for soccer to have a team with the star power we showcased, but we needed to make the most of that talent. I'd always said, it's no use having Beckham and Donovan if you don't have the right mix around them. We liked our chances in 2010 of winning it all, but in the Western Conference finals, Dallas beat us 3–0 before a home crowd of twenty-seven thousand at the Home Depot Center, and our season was over. For the second year in a row, we'd almost gotten there but fallen short. The headline in the morning *Los Angeles Times* that thumped against my front door in Manhattan Beach the next morning was a little dramatic, but true enough: "Galaxy Has a Long Time to Wait for Redemption."

The following January, David Beckham was over in England working out with Tottenham Hotspur, which at the time was in fourth place in the English Premier League. David was enjoying it. He'd always been very open with us, saying that he loved playing for Galaxy but also made a priority of representing England in international competition and that to stay sharp he liked to mix in time playing in Europe. The *Los Angeles Times* headline on January 4, 2011, was straightforward enough: "Tottenham Asks About Beckham." Yes, they did ask about having us loan David to them for two and a half months, until just before the MLS season began. We were fine about having David train with Tottenham, even if meant missing some of our preseason exhibition games and training camp. As a boy, he'd trained with Tottenham, before joining Manchester United, and it sharpened his game to be out there on the pitch with players like Robbie Keane, who at the time was captain of the Republic of Ireland national team. Robbie was a player whose game I'd always liked. Born in Dublin, he'd played in Italy when he was young, then had a good run with Tottenham for six years up until 2008. He went to Liverpool, but it didn't work out for him, so he was back at Tottenham again, trying to find a place for himself.

That August, we had an event with some of our Galaxy sponsors in the bowling alley at L.A. Live, an entertainment complex downtown, next to the Staples Center. As that was wrapping up, Tim Leiweke called to suggest we meet downstairs at Katsuya. It was clear what Tim wanted to discuss. We both knew we needed another player.

"One player I like is Robbie Keane," I said about halfway through our first bottle. "I think there's a chance. He had a falling out at Tottenham."

I didn't know. If it was obvious that Robbie wanted to make a move, then a lot of clubs would have been calling right then. Tim was intrigued. He thought highly of Robbie Keane as well.

"Bruce was clever to look for disgruntled players who could fit our league," Tim remembers. "Robbie was perfect for our league. He was a fierce competitor. He knew how to score goals. He could sing, he has an incredible voice, he could dance better than most human beings, he was a colorful character, but he knew how to win."

As we were talking, Tim pulled out his phone.

"I know Daniel Levy," he said. "I'll give him a call right now."

Daniel Levy was the chairman at Tottenham, and besides being known to this day as a hard guy to deal with, he lived in England, which was eight time zones away.

"Tim, you can't call him now!" I said. "It's like eight o'clock at night here, so it's three or four in the morning in England."

Tim just smiled.

"Daniel never sleeps," he told me.

The next thing I knew, he had Daniel on the phone. Daniel was in Florida, so it wasn't even midnight yet where he was.

"We have an interest in Robbie Keane," Tim told Daniel. "Who's the agent?"

Next we called the agent and said we were interested. We might have been into a second bottle of wine by then.

Tim called me the next day. "We can get Robbie," he said.

He'd talked to the agent. There was still a lot of hurried negotiation to get through. Tim remembers being with his wife, who needed X-rays, and having to step outside onto Wilshire Boulevard to juggle calls with Phil Anschutz, to make sure everything sounded good to him, with me, with Daniel Levy, and with Robbie's agent. The whole deal came together in forty-eight hours.

Within a week Robbie was in LA. We were very fortunate in our timing. Robbie, thirty-one, was looking to make a move and had heard good things about playing for LA Galaxy from Beckham when he was with Tottenham earlier in the year. It's not often you get a crack at a player of that caliber, who had scored more than 250 goals in his career by then, tenth all time in scoring in the Premier League at that time.

"People forget, Robbie Keane was one of the top goal scorers in the history of the English Premier League," Tim remembers.

"It's amazing we were able to get Robbie Keane on a team with David Beckham and Landon Donovan."

"I certainly had a good feeling about this move," Keane said at his welcome press conference on August 20. "I played in the Premiership for a long, long time and scored a lot of goals there. I just felt it was time for a new challenge. For me, it was an easy decision."

At the same press conference, Tim was unapologetic about going for the best. "We don't mind having a target on our back," he said. "My message to the rest of the league is, 'If you don't like it, go get your own.'"

Winning is all about building a team, and when it clicks, you know it right away. It clicked right away with Robbie, really from his first game with us. Here's how the *Los Angeles Times* described it that August 21:

> It took the Irish striker less than a half-hour to endear himself to Galaxy fans with a nifty goal in the twenty-first minute of a 2–0 victory over rival San Jose. But it was the celebration afterward that earned him points with fans. After giving the Galaxy a 1–0 lead, Keane cartwheeled his way to the southwest corner of the field as he has done for fourteen years. Then after receiving several leaping hugs, the newest member of the Galaxy took a moment to himself. Keane stood in the corner of the pitch and thrust his arms into the air, looking for a moment like a rock star who just finished his encore. He held his triumphant pose for a few seconds and then galloped down the sideline to the cheers of a crowd that was beside itself with Irish fever. Welcome to Los Angeles, Mr. Keane.

It was great theater, and it was great soccer. The fans loved it, and so did the players and my coaching staff. And so did I.

"We're elated with Robbie," I said after the game. "We had a great seventy minutes tonight and we think there's a lot of great games ahead for Robbie and our team."

There were. Robbie fit in just perfectly with the team, both in the locker room and on the field, and we could tell from the outset that at thirty-one he was still playing very well. He was a very competitive guy, and very creative. He had a wicked sense of humor. He was a real ball buster, which broke the ice immediately. But the main thing was, he had an unbelievable working relationship on the field with Landon and Beckham. It was as if they'd all been playing together for years.

"David and Robbie had a unique partnership from day one and a really tight friendship," says Tim. "They had both played in the English Premier League; they had both played in Europe; they had both played on a huge stage. There was a bond between them."

The thing to understand about Robbie was, he loved to play. Every day in training, he liked to go hard and play. So I made what adjustments I could to see that training went along his lines. Robbie never wanted to do fitness work; he never wanted to do any running, especially not a long run, that was for sure, but he could play for five hours. So we kind of disguised his fitness training. As long as there was a ball there, he would do it. You get creative in finding ways to get him where you want him to be. Whatever works, right?

The team by then was having a lot of fun on the field and off. I'm glad to think I helped them do that. As Tim says,

That run we had, and the chemistry we created, and the fun we had—that was a wonderful thing to be a part of. We just believed we were going to win. There was an air of confidence. They were not afraid of the high, lofty standards we had created for that group. Bruce did an amazing job of

taking those personalities and meshing them into a team. It was a good learning example, especially with the book and some of the crap that came out with the book, guys don't ultimately have to be the best friends to be champions. Bruce taught us that. He created a culture where we put that aside and fought for something together. That was, I think, his best work, the ability to get beyond the damn personalities.

Once it became more fun, everyone could enjoy each other more. David used to make a point of doing little things just to show he cared about his teammates. He's been close friends with the actor Tom Cruise for years, and he'd bring Tom by the locker room after a game, or we'd all meet for a drink. I'm not one to be starstruck. You do what I do, you meet all kinds of people. But Tom is just a really good guy, always fun to talk to. I thought he was great in *Born on the Fourth of July*, a 1989 Oliver Stone movie, which tells the real-life story of Ron Kovic, a Long Island guy who came back from the Vietnam War in a wheelchair and then became an activist. I got to know him later, and told Tom about it.

"He used to hang out with our summer lacrosse team," I told Tom.

"Really?" he said, doing that thing where he cocks his head a little and smiles.

Landon, who as team captain was always looking out for the guys, appreciated David's thoughtfulness. "If he had endorsements for something, the guys would come in to the locker room one morning and there would be a piece of clothing or a watch or an invite to a cool movie premiere that he had available to him that the rest of us wouldn't have had," Landon remembers. "I think he really enjoyed that. And David was really good about having guys get together on the road. He would invite guys to dinner, and he would pay for dinner."

Landon enjoyed the celebrity visits as well.

"Tom Cruise, Kobe Bryant, Wayne Gretzky—those guys aren't showing up unless David Beckham is there," Landon says now.

I don't know about that. They'd have come out to see Landon as well, I'm sure. There was an excitement around the team, and you learned to go with it. Getting fans excited about your team, and about Major League Soccer, wasn't just about having great players who could score goals they'd replay on ESPN; it was important also to generate some buzz. Generally if you look like you're having a great time, people are curious and want to check out what's going on. That was part of Tim's vision, to have a blast promoting the sport and the team and the players, and it was a good one. The mayor of Berlin, Germany, once said of his city "We are poor—but sexy." There was some of that to soccer at that time. Compared to the other major US sports leagues, we might have been poor—but we had our own appeal. Tim figured if the Super Bowl had turned into basically the biggest party of the year in the US, why not try to do that with the MLS Cup as well?

"We took the MLS Cup to the next level," Tim says. "Not just in importance, but the way we went about the week of the game. Bruce understood the parties, the corporate events. We wanted to act more like the NFL. Bruce got it. He totally got what we were trying to do for the league and the sport."

With Robbie in the mix, we made it back to the MLS Cup final against Houston Dynamo and this time won it, 1–0, on a Landon Donovan goal in the seventy-second minute set up by David Beckham and Robbie Keane. That goal was beautiful in many ways, especially for the teamwork it represented.

Landon and David had long since earned each other's respect as both great soccer players and great competitors, but that game stood out, because David was not only playing that whole season with a slightly fractured spine, but also he tore his right hamstring in practice the week before the final and still gave it his all. No question, that inspired the other guys, including Landon.

"He played on one leg," Landon said after the game. "He put in a warrior-like effort. [That] inspired me a lot."

I'd enjoyed working with David from day one and found him just the consummate soccer professional. He was someone you never worried about. He was always going to be a competitor, both in practice and on game day.

"I've been around great athletes and competitors in different sports in my life," I said after the game. "This guy is as good as it comes. He has an unbelievable desire to win and compete. David's a champion."

It was the third MLS Cup in franchise history for the Galaxy, my third MLS Cup after two with DC United, and the culmination of David's five-year contract with the Galaxy. We'd won the conference each of his last three seasons and had the best record in the league. Now he'd finally done what he came across the Atlantic to do, and he was thrilled. "If we didn't win tonight, it would have been an unsuccessful five years," he said after the game.

We made the announcement in May 2012 that David had signed a new contract to stay with the team, and that was the same month the Galaxy visited the White House as winners of the MLS Cup; I'm not gonna lie, that's kind of fun. My first time at the White House came after one of my University of Virginia teams won the national championship and Senator Harry Reid, whose son played for me at UVA, helped set up a visit when Bill Clinton was president. He looked tired; I could see that, looking across his desk at him in the Oval Office, and he was about to go through a difficult period of his presidency, but I'll never forget how he composed himself and went out to the Rose Garden for the ceremony and just came alive. He lit up the place. He was amazing.

I actually first met President George W. Bush back in 1978. His younger brother Marvin was an English major at UVA, and George came to a party with him that I attended, out in the country somewhere. I met George when he was one of the guys, and he always struck me as really decent. He called me a few times over the years. I really like him, and he's obviously a great sports fan.

Meeting President Obama that day with the Galaxy, there was an electricity. You could see that the president had prepared and that he and his wife, Michelle, were excited to be hosting a team that included David Beckham. Obama is absolutely wonderful. I think the world of him. He turned an ordinary hello-and-congratulations White House event into a kind of celebrity roast and clearly had a great time doing it.

He stood up at a podium with the White House seal and called us the Miami Heat of soccer, talked about Robbie Keane, and then said,

> *We also have a young up-and-comer on the team, a guy named David Beckham. I have to say, I gave David a hard time. I said half his teammates could be his kids. We're getting old, David. Although you're holding up better than me. Last year at the age of thirty-six, David had his best year in MLS, leading the team with fifteen assists. He did it despite fracturing his spine halfway through the season and injuring his hamstring the week before the championship game. He is tough. In fact, it is a rare man who can be that tough on the field and also have his own line of underwear. David Beckham is that man.*

The guys all grinned or laughed. The president also singled out Landon, who may even have earned a louder cheer. "Then there is the captain, Landon Donovan, who has done more for American soccer than just about anybody. Landon's eye for the net, his will to win, are legendary, and once again he stepped up when his teammates needed him most."

It was just a photo op really, but there's something about having a president you respect telling you, "You lived up to the hype." That was pretty cool.

Late that year we were back for another MLS Cup championship, and again it was a wild week. Our joyride of recent seasons was coming to an end, and we all knew it. We hosted the final at the Home Depot Center in Carson, which meant we had the whole LA area as a backdrop for a week of training, press conferences, and parties. David had announced late in the season that this would be his last in MLS, and we wanted to finish his amazing run with us on a high note. Whatever the naysayers had said early on, in the end no one could doubt that the Beckham Experiment was a roaring success. Galaxy had produced some of the best teams in the history of the league, and MLS had surged in growth, going from twelve to nineteen teams, getting ten new soccer-only stadiums built, and more than doubling its overall attendance. I was proud of the role I played in getting more people excited about soccer.

"David coming along gave us a chance to create, to brand, and to generate interest on a whole different level," Tim Leiweke says now. "David on his own would have brought a buzz, but it might not have been a brilliant success as to a product. We needed Bruce to get to that point, that partnership, along with Landon, and along with Robbie. Bruce had a very good run of it with, until now, the best team the league had ever seen."

The 2014 MLS Cup final was a rematch with Houston. Omar Gonzalez, our first Galaxy draft pick, played a strong game for us and scored our first goal. The Dynamo had taken an early one-goal lead, but we scored three times in the second half to win going away. Landon and Robbie Keane both converted penalty kicks, and once again we were MLS champs, despite having had to struggle through adversity much of the season, missing many of our best players, and despite falling behind in the MLS Cup final. "Thank God I had thirty-five years under my belt to be able to deal with this," I said afterward, thrilled but exhausted.

It took us two years to win one more MLS Cup for the Galaxy. In August 2014, Landon announced that he'd be retiring after the season. I'd followed his whole career, going back to those days when he was a young punk in Florida trying to outplay my DC United guys, and I couldn't have been prouder of all he'd done for soccer in this country. It wasn't always easy, carrying that weight, and yet Landon was always himself, always genuine, and he was always moving forward as a person. As Sam Borden wrote in the *New York Times*:

> *Donovan, more than any other player in American soccer history, was his country's heartbeat. He worked wonders with the ball, to be sure, but it was always more than that with Donovan. He did not just shine for the United States; he guided it. . . . Donovan has long been the face of American soccer and, like Michael Jordan in basketball, he will remain one of its icons even in retirement. His legacy is one of originality, of experimentation; he was a trailblazer, but by necessity. Donovan did not follow any one path to mainstream sports stardom in the United States, but that was, at least in part, because there was no obvious path for a soccer player to follow. Donovan turned professional in 1999 and will retire in 2014; in other words, he began his career when soccer in the United States was a test kitchen and will finish it with his sport a well-established restaurant.*

Does that make me a chef? I'll take that, I guess. The 2014 MLS Cup final was at home for us again, and our first goal was scored by Gyasi Zardes, who was born in nearby Hawthorne and played college soccer at Cal State Bakersfield. New England tied it up in the seventy-ninth minute, and then it was Robbie Keane who scored the game winner for us in overtime. It was an exciting win, my fifth MLS Cup as coach and third with the Galaxy, and a great way to send Landon off.

Here's how the *Los Angeles Times* summed it up:

> *For the last decade, the Galaxy has been Landon Donovan's team. And it has been a successful relationship, with the Galaxy winning four Major League Soccer titles under his leadership. But Sunday, late in overtime in the final game of Donovan's record-setting career, the team changed owners. Because when Robbie Keane capped a most-valuable-player season by scoring the winning goal in a 2–1 victory over the New England Revolution in the MLS Cup final at StubHub Center, the Galaxy became his. It was a smooth transition, with Donovan riding happily into retirement at thirty-two with six league championships, the same as Michael Jordan in the NBA and one more than Derek Jeter in Major League Baseball, while Keane claimed his third championship in three-and-a-half seasons in MLS.*

"I can't say enough about Robbie," I said afterward. "He's been a special leader, a great player, and a great friend and teammate."

The Call Comes

I had a good idea I was going to be hired again as US men's coach, taking over from Jürgen Klinsmann, long before it was widely known. How did I know that? Simple, I was offered the job. In fact, if not for a serious medical situation that put everything else on hold, I'd have taken over the national team by May 2016, instead of November 2016, a full six months earlier.

I met with Sunil Gulati and Dan Flynn, CEO of US Soccer, in April 2016 to talk about the future of the team and issues with the program. This was in Chicago a couple of months before Copa América Centenario. Sunil, Dan, and I agreed that I would be coming back as coach. They said it was time for a change.

Sunil was trying to get a deal done without my agent getting involved. It's true, Motzkin can be tough. He's a guy you want on your side, not across the negotiating table.

"Listen, Sunil, we basically have a deal, but my agent has to look at this contract," I said.

We decided Dan and I would talk the next day at one p.m. my time to move forward with talks. The next day came, and I didn't hear from Dan, except for a brief note saying he was probably going to have to delay our talk.

Later in the day, I heard from Jay Berhalter, number three at US Soccer, who told me, "Dan's gone." No one knew what was going on. Dan had disappeared and everyone was in the dark about what had happened.

Dan had played college soccer at Saint Louis University under the great Harry Keough, so he was a former athlete, but he was sixty-one by then, so we're talking about forty years earlier. I knew he'd had some heart issues, but I had no idea how serious they were. It turns out Dan was going to die if he did not get a heart transplant. He was on the list, and when you're on the list, and you get the call, you go! It's that simple. You have four hours to get there and have the surgery or you miss out on the opportunity and drop down the list.

So just after Sunil and Dan and I had a meeting to decide I'd be taking over the US team, Dan got the call—and he went! He flew from Chicago to Kansas City, and the next day, April 26, he had heart transplant surgery, which was fully successful. Dan's wife was in touch with me, giving me updates, and I was texting her back wishing Dan the best of luck. He was looking at eight weeks of recovery before he could come back to work, and with heart transplants, you want to be very careful about any potential complications.

"None of us even knew," Jay told me later. "Dan just left. He told nobody in soccer."

I felt a little bad for Sunil. He wanted to make a change and replace Klinsmann, but he was nervous about pulling the trigger. The timing was already going to be awkward, with Copa América coming up in June. Now Dan was gone for two months. It didn't feel right to move ahead at that time.

"Listen, Sunil, do you feel uncomfortable about this?" I said on the phone. "Forget about it. Don't worry about it."

Events had already been set in motion, though. This was a serious enough job offer that I felt it was only right to let the

Galaxy know what was happening, so I talked to the Galaxy of-
ficers, and there was back-and-forth between US Soccer and the
Galaxy. That set off a chain reaction. Up until then, not a lot of
preparation had gone into how the Galaxy would move on when
I left. Since I was both general manager and head coach, coming
up with a plan to replace me might have been a little more complicated than they'd thought. So when the move came to a crashing halt, all because of Dan Flynn's heart, and I gave the Galaxy
the news I'd actually be staying, it was a little awkward. They
were happy that they weren't losing me, but I also had the feeling
they were a little pissed off that I was contemplating moving on.
So I raised the point with them.

"Why *wouldn't* I take that job again?" I asked them.

Coaching your country's national team is a great experience.
It's a great responsibility and a great challenge, but it's also a
great honor. I'm proud to stand out there on the sideline for the
national anthem and cheer on the red, white, and blue.

Probably the timing was good. Maybe I'd have even been smart
to wrap up my time with the Galaxy sooner. We'd accomplished
so much and had such a great time doing it that at some point my
energy was going to flag. Maybe energy is the wrong way to put
it. I'm always energetic. I always put in the work. But if it's not
quite as fun, not quite as exciting, there might be a spark of in-
spiration that doesn't kick in quite the same way. I've said repeat-
edly that we were lucky it all worked out so well having Landon
Donovan, David Beckham, and Robbie Keane playing together.
It wasn't always going to work out so well.

We still had Robbie Keane in 2016, and I can't say enough
about everything he brought to the team. In 2015 we'd also added
Steven Gerrard to the mix. Steven, a great midfielder for many
years with the English national team and Liverpool of the English
Premier League, had a tough year in 2014. Liverpool was in first
place in the Premier League that April by five points but suffered

a 2–0 loss to Chelsea when Gerrard slipped and fell to set up the first Chelsea goal. Liverpool ended up being overtaken by Manchester City. Gerrard had scored so many goals, won so many games, but everyone kept talking about that slip.

"It's probably been the worst three months of my life," Gerrard told reporters that July. "I've seen it a few times. I don't have to watch something like that to go through the pain again and again and again. . . . When something like that happens you have to face up and be man enough to take it on the chin. Accept it happened. You can't change it. I haven't lost my man at a set-piece. I haven't missed a penalty. I haven't made a bad pass or a mistake. That's why it was cruel. Every single person on the planet slips at some point in their life, whether it is on a set of stairs, on the floor or whatever."

We were happy to give Steven a fresh start with Galaxy. He'd played seventeen seasons with Liverpool, scoring 182 goals in 696 games, and also scored 21 goals for England in 114 appearances and for years served as team captain. He joined the Galaxy in July 2015, and we hoped for the same kind of magic that adding Robby Keane had given us, but the team faltered that season. Robby had another strong year, leading us with 20 goals, but we finished in fifth place and made it only to the MLS quarter-finals.

I mentioned earlier that often the hardest challenge as a coach is in dealing with great players at the tail end of their careers. Steven was a champion, used to winning, but in his time with us we had trouble making the most of his talents. He was with us a year and a half but was limited to thirty-four appearances over that time, scoring five goals and adding fourteen assists. Really it came down to injuries; that was why Steven had a tough run with the Galaxy. In his last couple of years at Liverpool, he worked with a manager who catered to his age and experience in an effort to get the best out of him. With the Galaxy, it was hard to find the right balance because of his injuries. When Steven trained less, he was not as effective and fit. When he trained more and played, he eventually broke down. A remarkable career took its toll on his body, and he was physically limited at the end. Regardless, I never questioned that it was a good move to get him for the Galaxy. Sometimes those moves just don't work out as well as you hope they will.

The most interesting thing that happened with the Galaxy in 2016 was the return of Landon Donovan that September. It all started as a joke. Landon was working our game with Vancouver as a TV analyst and was talking to some of our people about the rash of injuries that hit us, including to Steven Gerrard, Jelle Van Damme, and Gyasi Zardes, and someone asked Landon if he was ready to suit up and take the field for us. We could use the help!

Landon laughed off the suggestion, but then thought about it some more. He hadn't played in nearly two years and didn't think he could pick up where he'd left off. But if he could help us, he was game to try. So he and I sat down to talk it over. We agreed that we had to keep expectations down, and Landon had to understand I'd be using him in whatever way I thought would help the team. He was fully on board with that, so I talked it over with my staff and team officials and we all said, *Why not?* Landon was happy, enjoying fatherhood, and loved the idea of having his son on the field.

"I know this won't be received well by everyone," he wrote in a September post on Facebook, thanking his fans. "I can't tell you how much I appreciate each and every one of you. I've been fortunate to lead an incredible life, and I can't wait to be on the field again and hear your cheers. Also, as all you parents know, having a child is truly a life-changing experience. Nothing would make me happier than standing on the field with Talon and the rest of my family celebrating the Galaxy's 6th championship on December 10th. I will do everything in my power to make that happen, and I hope we are all there celebrating together!"

It didn't work out that way. We finished in third that year and were knocked out in the semifinals of the Western Conference playoffs again, but Landon's return did give us some energy. He scored a goal in one of his first games back. We were down to Sporting Kansas City late in the game. I subbed in Landon in the seventy-fourth minute, and two minutes later he scored a left-footed goal to tie it up. His first four appearances were all as a reserve, as he and I had discussed before we decided to give it a try, but he started in Houston on October 16 and started again at home for the last regular-season game, getting his legs back in time for the playoffs. "That was really the first time I felt like I was a normal soccer player again," he said afterward. Too bad we weren't able to get back to another MLS Cup final to see what Landon could do.

The Galaxy season was over by the first week of November, just before the US men's national team started its bid to qualify for the World Cup in Russia with a November 11 home game against Mexico and then a trip to Costa Rica to take on the Ticos in San Jose on November 15. The Mexico game would be played in Columbus, Ohio, where we have a lot of our World Cup qualifiers for the simple reason that, unlike in New York or many other spots in the country, we can count on having a vocal majority of US fans, which may sound like a given but often isn't, demoralizingly enough.

That game had a particular undercurrent. As the *New York Times* put it beforehand, "While only a few hundred fans of Mexico are expected to be in the stadium—they are generally allocated a place in the corner of the upper deck—the atmosphere could be especially charged because the game will be played just three days after an Election Day in which Mexico, and Mexican-Americans, have been thrust into a prominent place by the Republican Party nominee, Donald J. Trump."

Whether Trump's victory in the election had any impact on

the proceedings in Columbus is impossible to know, but I'll just assume no. Four times in row, US teams had taken care of business on home soil against Mexico in World Cup qualifiers, each time winning 2–0. But it took only twenty minutes to establish that that pattern was not going to repeat itself, when Mexico scored first to shock the host Americans. Bobby Wood scored in the forty-ninth minute to tie it up. For the US team, a tie at home would have been a disappointment and a setback, but not a catastrophe. That's where it looked like it was going, and then in the final minute before stoppage time, Rafael Márquez scored to give Mexico a 2–1 victory.

That was bad, but what happened to the US team four days later in Costa Rica was closer to horrific. Here's how Sam Borden's *New York Times* obituary read:

The defense was a shambles. The midfield had little presence. The attack, such as it was, just spun and sputtered. How bad was it? It is difficult to know where to start. There was no fluidity from the United States national team here on Tuesday night against Costa Rica. No flow, no rhythm, no concentrated push, either early or late. There was no sturdiness or stoutness or resilience in a game that felt critical. There was no creativity.

Mostly, there were a lot of mistakes. And moments of confusion. And missed passes. There were also, understandably, a lot of goals, though all of them were for Costa Rica, as the Ticos—pounded by the United States earlier this year during the Copa América—shredded the Americans, 4–0, in a World Cup qualifying result that could reasonably be labeled the single worst performance during Coach Jürgen Klinsmann's tenure. Never before has the United States lost the first two games of the six-team final qualifying round known as the hexagonal, but after a 2–1 defeat to Mexico

last Friday in Ohio, the Americans will have to wait four
months to play again—knowing all the while that, with
zero points, they are tied for last place.

I had trouble watching the Costa Rica game. Seriously. It was
uncomfortable for me to see the US team playing that way, out
of sync and at odds with one another, looking as though they
really didn't care all that much. You never know from the outside
looking in what's happening with a team, and it's never smart to
pretend you do, never smart to criticize without knowing all the
internal dynamics. But really when it gets that bad, the internal
dynamics don't matter. Those back-to-back losses were a a fiasco
for US soccer, and no matter how much of the blame lay at Klinsmann's feet, it was clear he'd coached his last game for the US.

Having been offered the job months earlier, I knew what was
coming. Sunil reached out again that month, and he and I met at
LAX to talk over how to proceed.

"All right, no agent, here's the deal," he said, and went over a
few things, then added, "You good? That's it?"

I did a kind of Columbo thing, not answering at first.

"Well, there are a couple of issues," I said.

So we talked some more, and ultimately I kicked it over to
Motzkin, my agent. It wasn't about haggling over a few dollars.
I was always about the challenge, not money, and that's even
more true later on in life, having already done all that I've done
in coaching. But sometimes you have to lay the groundwork for
things to work, and that means making sure that an offer is fully
respectful and both parties are responsive. So my agent needed to
be involved. There's always a hassle or two along the way. That's
why they call it negotiation. Then everything was wrapped up,
and I was thrilled to be back in the saddle.

The official announcement on Klinsmann came on November 21. I like Jürgen, and there's no question that in pushing the

program forward in many ways, he made my job easier. We travel now in a way that's much more comfortable for the players, for example, and that's a huge plus. In addition, the program is supported in all areas to a degree we couldn't have dreamed about years ago.

Here's how Jürgen's final days as coach played out, as recorded by the *New York Times*:

> *On Thursday, Jürgen Klinsmann, the coach of the United States national men's soccer team, dined with President Obama, Chancellor Angela Merkel of Germany, a number of Nobel laureates and a couple of astronauts at a gala in Berlin. The sausages were "excellent," he said.*
>
> *On Friday, Klinsmann returned to his home in California and was bemused by the criticism he was receiving in the news media for two recent losses by his team, which had damaged—but not erased—its chances of qualifying for the 2018 World Cup. On Sunday, Klinsmann aggressively defended his record as coach in an interview, saying that he was "very comfortable" in his position and was not especially concerned about being removed.*
>
> *On Monday, Klinsmann was fired.*

And on Tuesday, Sunil held a press conference to announce me as the new coach, saying, "I don't view it as 'Bruce 2' but more of 'Bruce 2.0.' He has far more experience than he did when he had the national team the first go-around."

That was true enough.

"I never expected to be back in this role the way it came about over the last forty-eight hours," I said at the press conference. "The game in Costa Rica was certainly disappointing for the group. Hopefully, it's one that allows us to step back and evaluate what went well and what didn't go well in that game and hopefully it's something that we can use for the betterment of the team as we move forward, in how to be prepared and play games on the road in CONCACAF. Obviously, it was a disappointing result. The only thing I can tell you is that we're going to make it better."

I talked about what I've gained as a coach with more experience:

I've learned a lot. I've had ten years on the field at the club level, and I've had the opportunity to work with some of the most talented players in the world and understand how they work and how to build a team. And I've continued to grow on the tactical side, continued to grow in learning how to deal with players and learning how to plan when playing away and playing in big matches. I think ten years later I'm better prepared for this job than I was in 1998 and 2002, and ultimately 2006. I'm hopeful that the experiences that I have are going to benefit the program. You know, one of the things you learn from experience is, you see things a lot clearer and a lot quicker than you did previously, and the game has slowed down a bit where I can see as a coach, and in my position, how things are happening on the field. I'm better at identifying the strengths and weaknesses of players and I think I'm better at how you build a team. Certainly, this time around it's going to be a great challenge. I'm excited about it.

Part IV

Disappointment on the Road to Russia

A Game of Catch-up

You can never let time feel like your enemy. Time's just time. It doesn't speed up or slow down based on your needs; it does its own thing. Taking over as US coach again when I did, I was behind the eight ball. We had no margin for error, having lost two games already in the Hex, with only eight left. I needed to shift the way our players thought and felt about the program and playing for the national team, and I needed to build for the future, all at once. I needed to accomplish things that take years, but I had only months to do it. If I'd taken the attitude that I had to hurry up, like someone running around and talking too fast all the time, I'd have been screwed. If I'd shown even a hint of panic, I'd also have lost before I even started. That would have spread like wildfire. Instead, I had to accept that I wasn't going to have time to do everything I'd like to have done. I'd need to focus on a few main priorities and do my best to nail them, then trust that I was setting in motion the potential for good things to happen. You set it all up, knowing you've done all that needs doing, and then you wait to see how it turns out.

I'm usually not that impressed with the level of insight I see in sportswriters. I understand, they have a tough job, trying to keep readers interested with behind-the-scenes details, even though they don't get much access, and trying to keep feeding the social-media beast even as they try to pay attention to the fine points during the games. It's got to be hard to watch the game closely when you're bending over, sending out something on Twitter or Facebook or whatever. The kind of sportswriter I most admire is someone like George Vecsey, longtime sports columnist for the *New York Times*, now semi-retired, who was actually a *Times* correspondent in Appalachia in the early 1970s, covering coal-mine disasters and poverty and even country music. He also loved soccer. I'd say he had it about right in summing up my approach when taking the job again in November 2016.

"The once and future coach—Bruce Arena—will try to make it sound simple," Vecsey wrote then in a *Times* column. "Even at sixty-five, he will roll his eyes and sneer at complicated questions about strategy and formations. This masks his feel of the game, buys him time and distance. Don't overthink it—that's the message, conveyed in a Lawn Guyland accent that he blessedly has never lost in his wanderings. . . . He will no doubt try to simplify the task of resurrecting the wretched national team after its 4–0 walking surrender at Costa Rica last week. US Soccer, which removed Jürgen Klinsmann as coach on Monday, on Tuesday appointed Arena—the best person on the planet for the job at this point."

Simple was the way to go to avoid making it even harder on yourself. When you pick up a team in the middle of the cycle, you're inheriting someone else's team, not necessarily building your own. Of course, you're doing both, but at a deeper level, in terms of the fundamental architecture, you have to go with what has been built whenever possible. One mistake a lot of coaches would make in that situation is to do what sportswriters often do, which is to be too impatient to get to the bottom of a riddle.

Experience gives you more patience, and you're less interested in whether you're right or wrong in what you think you know and more interested in putting in the time to take a deeper look at key questions.

A good example was the European question we faced with the team. I made it an early priority to fly to Europe to do everything I could to improve my relationships with players based in Europe, whether players like Fabian Johnson and John Brooks, who grew up in Germany speaking mostly German, or US-born players like Christian Pulisic and Bobby Wood, also playing in the Bundesliga. These were all important players to us. We needed to have good communication with them and, just as important, with their clubs, and we needed to understand how they saw their situations and what it meant to them to compete with the US national team. I've been around enough—visited enough countries around the world, twenty-five in all—to understand that cultural differences can play out in ways that lead to misunderstandings. The German mentality is just different, a little more reserved. What we see as vital passion and commitment they might at times see as a little too rah-rah, words rather than actions, but for a US team, which needs to play with fierce passion to make up for some other shortcomings, being a little reserved is never going to cut it. My approach has always been about building a team on which all players have a sense of being a part of something larger than themselves, and some passion and fiery intensity are what you need to get that going.

It's not complicated, and yet the press generally has little time for the questions that really matter. I did a session with reporters in late November 2016 about taking over again as US coach and had to wade through the predictable silly questions about analytics. Sometimes reporters are like the kind of students who want to make sure you know they've done the required reading, as opposed to just keeping their eyes open and asking a question they really want answered. Advanced analytics, for the time be-ing, are a joke when it comes to soccer. I'm open to that changing in the future, as data-gathering expands in ways we can't even imagine now, but unlike baseball, for example, soccer is not a sport in which analytics are going to offer an improvement on what your eyes tell you if you just watch closely with a knowledge of the game. One reason numbers are misleading is that there are a thousand factors to keep in mind—game conditions, heat or cold, team leading or trailing, a man up or a man down, and on and on—and also that they don't tell you anything about what goes into a performance. The challenge is doing everything you can to get players ready to play at the highest level and also trying to limit unpredictability. That's how you build a winning team, once you've assembled the right mix of players.

"We, and countries around the world, have players who are spotty," I told reporters bluntly in late November 2016. "There are too many peaks and valleys of players. We've got to level out their performance." One way you try to do that is to focus not just on *your* players, but on everyone in US Soccer, whether their role seems small or large. They all matter, and how they work to-gether can make all the difference in generating the positive team chemistry you need. Taking over again that November, I wanted to make sure that everyone connected to US Soccer felt involved and motivated and included. This might sound obvious, but it's a factor that often gets overlooked or bypassed.

I always tried to follow that principle of inclusiveness. For ex-ample, I always loved being out on the field running a practice. It was fun! It took me back to all my earlier years out on a field with other athletes, trying to get it right. I liked the give and take, the feeling of excitement as we built toward something. I liked all of it, but there were days when I actively coached the team, and there were days when I sat back and watched. Sometimes I handed over running a practice to my assistants. That was important. I wanted them to feel challenged and to grow as young coaches; I wanted them to get every chance to contribute. If later they were out on their own as coaches in their own right, I wanted their time working with me to have helped them in every way possible. That was as true for my son, Kenny, as for anyone else. I was grateful to the Galaxy for being so cooperative in releasing me to join the national team—and also letting me bring my whole coaching staff with me, starting with Dave Sarachan, a former MLS Coach of the Year and a top head coach in his own right, as well as Kenny, who in 2012 in his first year as a head coach at the collegiate level, oversaw a resurgence at Florida International University, which recorded more wins than it had in seven years. As a *Los Angeles Times* headline put it, "US National Coach Bruce Arena Raids Galaxy Staff for Four Assistant Coaches."

Besides Dave and Kenny, I also brought with me Pat Noonan and Richie Williams. Pat and Richie were both former players, and both are very bright. I saw Pat as a future head coach, serious and a hard worker, who scouted opponents for us and worked with our forwards. Richie, who played for me back at UVA and DC United, and later led the U-17 residency program at Bradenton, was and is a good guy who loves to be on the field. Matt Reis, the goalkeeper coach, likewise remains quite a personality, funny and articulate. Daniel Guzman, the strength and conditioning coach, was just twenty-six then, bright and enthusiastic with a great future. His job was not only to work with players in the gym and on the field, but to monitor their fitness levels and injuries, from major to very minor, on a weekly basis.

My routine didn't change much in the new job. My office as Galaxy coach was in the StubHub Center in Carson, about ten miles from my home in Manhattan Beach, and my office as US team coach was also in the StubHub Center, just across the hall. Jürgen, for whatever reasons, did not spend a lot of time in those offices, and his coaches were in different places. That was how

I'd done it in my previous eight years as the national team coach as well. Our staff was spread out throughout the country, and I worked out of my home in Fairfax, Virginia.

Things had changed for the better, allowing us to be more efficient. We could track all of our players through the Internet, television, and a number of different applications, keeping up on performance analytics and scouting. We maintained contact with the players through various forms of communication, personal visits, contact with their clubs, and at times contact with their agents. We tried to stay on top of everything and had a lot of information to use to evaluate our players, letting us hope to select our best rosters for these critically important games.

I liked to have my guys together, and when I say guys, I mean my coaches and also my amazing assistant, Martha Romero, who was basically an extension of my brain. She was usually a step or two ahead of me, and believe me, I loved it. We'd worked closely since she started at the Galaxy in August 2008. She remembers walking in for her first day, playing it straight—and me making some wisecrack. She went with it. "I wouldn't have it any other way!" she says. She kept up with me, no matter how hard we were all working, whether for the Galaxy or the US team. "How he challenges his staff daily, myself included, continues to this day," she said recently.

We made some physical changes to the office to create more of a common area, and it paid off. Having a close-knit staff made the job more enjoyable, for one thing, and it also definitely encouraged creativity and initiative.

I think it's bad when one individual in a position of authority takes on too much control and is afraid to delegate. When I took over again as US coach, I told people to be responsible for their areas. "I'm not doing your job!" I said, and it was a case where a no-nonsense New York accent probably didn't hurt. "*You* do it."

Some were uneasy with that approach. They wanted me to

tell them what to do. I made clear what I would do and what I wouldn't do. I didn't need to review the details of who was rooming with whom on the road when I talked to our team administrator. "You guys figure it out," I said. I didn't need to hear every update from our medical staff. "Come to me with the important stuff. I trust you. I know you'll let me know when you need me in the loop on something."

You're building a team within the team and a team outside the team. It's important to realize that it's an organization and you need that organization to work *for* you, not against you, starting with Sunil and Dan Flynn at the top, whom I wanted involved. It was their team, not my team. I let them know what was going on as often as I could. Sometimes they might hear from me more than they wanted to hear from me, but overall they responded well and were cooperative and supportive. I can understand why people hire coaches to speak to corporations. The concept of a team is important, whether it's in a game or in business or in teaching or whatever. For me it was very important that our team included everyone and that everyone felt they were being respected and heard. I'm not always touchy-feely. If I see young kids being used as ball boys in an important World Cup qualifying match, I might bark out my objection. But people who work with me know I'm actually looking out for what's important to them, not just going through the motions. That's never been my way. I care if they're there. They're all part of a team. If there's something they're not doing right, I'll tell them. But I'm not doing their job. "*You* do it."

Nothing will be accomplished overnight. Over time you find out what kind of progress you're making. There's a process you've got to appreciate. Coming in, I was fortunate to know a lot of the players. I'd been coaching in the professional league and I'd known them for years, and a lot of these guys had played for me, which helped, but it's always challenging, because you need to have a complete and accurate sense of where any given player is on a given day. That's how you map out different possibilities.

In addition, the game has changed over the years. It's quicker and faster, and players are fitter and more athletic. But it hasn't changed that much. I've always believed in pressuring the ball, for example. That's become more applicable now in the modern game. At the international level, it's a little harder, because you're going against better players, but I think it's a style that's well suited for the American player, who is athletic, competitive, and fit and can apply sustained pressure. We thought about this imperative thirty, forty years ago, and it has come full circle; it's reality today.

My first training camp as US coach in more than ten years came in January 2017 in Southern California. Steven Goff of the *Washington Post* came to Phyllis's and my house to do a feature on me leading up to that camp, and he had a little fun at my expense (were the shorts *that* short?), which I always enjoy.

The items sitting on the second level of Bruce Arena's home tell not only his personal history, but help tell the American soccer story. An autographed ball from his goalkeeping days with the Tacoma Tides in 1976 and University of Virginia trading cards, the coach in short shorts. A photo with President Obama after another Los Angeles Galaxy championship and a pine crate of Opus One, high-end red wine, from David Beckham and family. Memorabilia from D.C. United's early days. Team pictures and books, medals and trophies. A closet holds additional treasures—markers on the timeline of an unmatched coaching career that, some forty years after it began, has taken an unforeseen spin. In November, 10 years after Arena's first tour as national team coach ended in disappointment, the US Soccer Federation called on him to steady a teetering act.

I talked with Goff about how important it was to me that the United States qualify for the World Cup in 2018, as we had every year since 1986. Qualifying is tough, it's bruising, and it's unpredictable, which is why we were one of only seven countries in the world—seven!—to have qualified every four years since 1986. Besides South Korea, which like the US was a team that relied on being fit and competing hard, the other five were all established world soccer powers: Argentina, Brazil, Germany, Italy, and Spain. For me, especially having coached the 2002 and 2006 teams, maintaining that legacy was uppermost—and falling short was unthinkable.

"It would be terrible," I told Goff. "How terrible? Are there different levels of terrible?"

Learning the Players

Our exercise in triage started with trying to improve our defense and team chemistry. We'd already conceded six goals in just two games of play in the Hex. I researched different rosters that had been used over the previous two years and had a difficult time finding rhyme or reason in the choices that had been made, making conclusions hard to come to. I thought the roster could be improved by addressing a shortage of outside backs and wide midfielders, and we needed better teamwork in simply passing the ball. I thought our pool of center backs, goalkeepers, and strikers was pretty solid. Still, things didn't add up. To me, this group should have been better than they were. The team needed to be "coached up," and having brought my entire staff over from the LA Galaxy, I felt comfortable that we could put in the work on and off the field to get the job done.

We began the process by creating a working pool of approximately seventy players. From this pool, we created a roster for our January 2017 camp and for friendlies versus Serbia and Jamaica, a group comprised mostly of MLS players. Out of this this camp we would blend in our players based in Europe and Mexico to form a roster for our critically important games on March 24 and 28 versus Honduras and Panama. These games would go a long way toward deciding if we would be positioned to qualify for the 2018 World Cup.

I still needed to look ahead to the Gold Cup, coming up in July; I was certain that our players abroad were going to need a break then. In addition, adding new faces to the program would be important if we did eventually qualify for the 2018 World Cup. There would certainly be a need to make some changes to our roster, and the experience gained by these players in 2017 could turn out to be very important.

With the exception of Jorge Villafaña, who played for Santos Laguna in Mexico, all of our players for that January camp were MLS-based. Most of them were coming off of breaks of four to twelve weeks, so there were significant fitness issues to deal with. We hoped to have them somewhat match fit by the end of the month, a goal that was close to impossible to accomplish. You do what you can, but in the end it's up to the players, and they did a great job in pushing one another. I had invaluable time getting to know them all and gaining an understanding of how they each fit in to the larger picture. Camp concluded with my first games back as coach, friendlies against Serbia on January 31 in San Diego and versus Jamaica in Chattanooga on February 3. We didn't do much against Serbia, playing to a scoreless draw, then picked up a 1–0 win over Jamaica (via a nice goal by Jordan Morris) that, given the US team's recent history, mattered more than a friendly should.

"The biggest thing we are trying to do is form a team out of this group of players, to take a little pride out of what they are doing," I said after the win over Jamaica. "We've had two games where we haven't conceded a goal. We can certainly get a few more goals."

I started the camp going into those two games hoping we could see if we could address the issue of outside backs and wide midfielders. Also, I wanted to see if we had a potential number-ten player. At the conclusion of camp, it was clear that our veteran players Michael Bradley, Jermaine Jones, Jozy Altidore, Nick Rimando, and Alejandro Bedoya would remain important players for our qualifiers in March. In addition, Graham Zusi demonstrated progress in a positional change at right back, and Villafaña showed promise at left back. In midfield, Darlington Nagbe and Sebastian Lletget stood out, as did forwards Jordan Morris and Juan Agudelo. Therefore, despite our form not being the greatest, the camp was productive in terms of finalizing a roster for the qualifiers in March and June, as well as the Gold Cup in July.

Once you've built the team *behind* the team, as I did, pretty quickly taking over the national squad again, you start to reach out to every player as an individual, but not with a particular agenda—you're just looking to build bridges and gain understanding. It's a slow process and not always a linear one. You might feel you're breaking through with a player—say, getting him to return your texts!—and then he gets hurt and goes off the grid and you have to start all over again. Above all, you can't expect your vision to resonate unless the team is showing progress, especially progress on the field.

In March 2017, we were back in San Jose, where I'd had so many big games in my time as a coach. The first game in the history of Major League Soccer—DC United versus the San Jose Earthquakes—had been held there. My first game as US national team coach had also been in San Jose, at the old football stadium used by San Jose State University, Spartan Stadium. Now it was back to San Jose, only we wouldn't be playing at Spartan Stadium this time. Marie Tuite, the athletic director at San Jose State, is a good friend of mine, and I love the school, but at least for the players and coaches, Spartan Stadium was never our first choice for soccer. Instead we'd be playing in the sleek new soccer-only stadium the Earthquakes had built right next to San Jose Airport, part of a wave of new facilities throughout the country that were transforming the look and feel of MLS games. Avaya Stadium, which opened in early 2015, has a distinct look, with the highest slant on seating in MLS, to give everyone a better view, and an open bar area along one entire end zone—it's called the largest open-air bar in North America (how that's judged I have no idea).

We came together for our training camp going into those two games, and I was just glad I had some background with some of these players. As the coach of a club team, you get to know all your players very well very fast because you're around them all the time, but coaching the national team is completely different. It's not easy building relationships when you see each other for a couple weeks at a time over the course of the year. My coaching staff was keeping up with guys, which helped, but nothing beats training together at a camp to learn more about each other. I needed the veterans to set a tone, and fortunately I'd known many of them for years.

Some people don't like Michael Bradley that much as a player, but I find him to be a tremendous team player. His leadership is invaluable, but he has to play well for his leadership to mean something, and he *has* played well. There was clearly a problem with Michael and Jürgen. Michael didn't think the team was prepared properly, and as the son of a coach, that ate him up. Having been around his dad all those years and played for his dad on the national team, Michael respected the fact that there are certain things you have to do with teams to get them right. He felt that under Klinsmann something had been lacking.

Michael Bradley is definitely a coach's son. He's going to be involved with the game the rest of his life, whether as a coach or in another role. He's not going to be selling cars when he's done playing, that's for sure. Michael is the spitting image, mentally, of his dad, Bob—the way he analyzes things and articulates them, his professional habits, and his seriousness all flow from his father's approach. Whatever he's lacking in pure talent, when he's on top of his game, his mental approach and physical preparation put him over the top. He reads the game well and communicates very well. He can win tackles and is good in the air, and he's a pretty solid passer. He plays for ninety minutes each and every game. That's what separates Michael from everyone else on that US squad.

There were other fine players I was lucky to work with. Tim Howard made his national team debut when I was coach in 2002, and I've always liked him as a player and had great respect for him as a person. He grew up with Tourette's syndrome—just imagine what he had to take from other kids—and developed into not just a first-rate goalkeeper but a first-rate human being as well. I give him a lot of credit for how he dealt with his experiences with Tourette's, especially in making it public.

Between 2006, when Tim was a backup on our World Cup team, and 2016, we had very little contact. We ran into each other now and then, said hello, and it was always positive, but we didn't talk much. When I took the US job a second time, Tim and I were in touch right away and had some great conversations. We've had a good relationship, and I have a lot of respect for him, as I hope he does for me.

Howard was phenomenal for the United States in the 2014 World Cup in Brazil, easily the MVP—without him, I don't know where we'd have been. The US was so bad in that World Cup, it was an absolute miracle they got out of group play. As they say, he stood on his head. The game against Belgium was scoreless after ninety minutes, and that was almost entirely due to Tim's play in goal—he made sixteen saves, the most in a World Cup game since records began being kept in 1966. Imagine the US winning that game and making it to the quarterfinal instead of losing 2–1 and being eliminated.

Tim deserved to have that team go through, and I understood it when he took some time off afterward. Then he had a tough break in the November 2016 World Cup qualifier against Mexico, tearing the adductor longus muscle in his groin area, requiring months to come back. Groin injuries can linger, so that was a challenging one for Tim. He eventually had surgery but still came into our camp to see the guys for a couple days in January 2017 in Los Angeles. He was an important leader for us in camp, helping set a tone for the other players.

Tim turned thirty-eight in March 2017. He had nothing to prove at that point in his career, but he was still highly motivated. It was wonderful to see. Being smart and experienced can help you make up for some physical decline, and as we have all seen over the years, Tim is very talented. He was in the thick of our plans for getting to Russia, and we'd have to make ongoing evaluations and determinations month by month to see where we were. For me, Tim was sure to be a vital part of the 2018 US team, no matter how much game action he saw, because he had such a fierce commitment to winning. He badly wanted the US team to be good, and he was fully committed to the process, and as I've said, that commitment is half the battle. With some of our guys in Germany, that was not always the case, so the hope was to have veterans like Tim pull them along as they spent more time together.

Another veteran coming back from health issues was Clint Dempsey, but in his case the important question was whether his life might be threatened, not just his playing career. He started having problems with his heart in early 2016 that eventually became noticeable enough to affect his ability to play. In August of that year, he was diagnosed with an irregular heartbeat and was out of action for the Seattle Sounders, who went on to win the MLS Cup even without him. But soccer took a backseat to life. I gave Clint a call in that period just to talk over how he was feeling. We'd known each other a long time, and I was concerned.

"I really appreciated that," Clint says now. "He was calling me when I was having the heart issues. I might not even have been able to come back or get to the same level again. Who knows what's going to happen when you're having two heart procedures? But to have him call and ask about things and to care, that meant a lot to me."

I was glad to be there for Clint. If you don't care about these guys as people, you're never going to be much of a coach, but it's more than that. You learn from each other along the way. We all have brushes with mortality, losing people close to us, running into health issues that could turn out to be serious, and how you respond to those brushes helps define who you are. Character matters in sports. Life experience matters in sports. For Clint, the heart issues gave him a new way of looking at things. He didn't *need* to be there, playing with us, but he burned with competitiveness.

Clint was cleared to start training again after I was back as US coach, and that winter, soon after I took the job, I reached out to him about joining the national team again. At that point we didn't know if Clint would ever be able to regain his fitness, but I wanted him training with us whether he could play again or not.

"I know you're coming back," I said. "If you'd like to come in, you can train when you feel like training, not be involved in any of the friendly games, whatever. We'd love to have you."

Dempsey was eventually cleared to play again and the decision was made that he should stay with Seattle in the preseason and slowly build his fitness back up. I called him again in February.

"Clint, we're keeping an eye, just to let you know," I said. "If you get through everything, I'm going to consider you for the roster in March."

Then by early March, he wasn't just *playing* for Seattle; he was starting and playing ninety minutes. He was back. So I called him again.

"We'd like to have you in to camp," I said. "We'll probably just play you short minutes in the games."

"Whatever you need," Clint said.

By the time he reported, he'd had three or four games for Seattle and was playing well. He looked good in camp, and it made sense to play him against Costa Rica and Panama. Clint was the same player he always was, in a good way, but you also saw that he was a different person. I think the heart condition allowed him to gain a deeper perspective. I think after that he greatly appreciated what he had. As an athlete and even as a coach, when things go well and you have some success and you're in a good place financially, sometimes you take things for granted. I think he was probably like that. And coming back from the heart issues, he really respected where he was in his life, both as a player and a person.

Goal scorers do their thing in a way you can't coach. For Clint, being at his best meant playing utterly without fear. What he'd been through seemed to help him make the most of every opportunity.

> It's going through a lot of ups and downs and a lot of grind to get to where you are, hitting a lot of walls and getting a lot of noes, and when you get your chance, you know that it might not come again. It's realizing that and knowing that if you're going to go down, go down being true to yourself, [better] than to try to not be true to yourself and go down anyway. I always had that mind-set: if I'm going to go, be successful or not be successful, it will kind of be on my own terms. Obviously you have to listen to the coach and adapt to his game, but still bring the things that caused you to fall in love with the game in the first place; otherwise you wouldn't be doing yourself justice or having as much fun.

National teams, even more than club teams, have to be led not only by the coach but by players as well. Veteran players like

Michael Bradley, Tim Howard, and Clint Dempsey can show younger players what it means to take the utmost pride in playing for the US and being committed to doing whatever it takes to make the team better. That commitment can rub off on young players like Christian Pulisic, whose talent and commitment were also strong but who needed experience and more games behind him to learn what goes into being a champion.

I felt good about our chances going against Honduras in San Jose on March 24. I liked our combination of youth and experience, I liked the confidence I'd been seeing in camp, and I knew we had to get a W or we were in trouble, so there would be no lack of urgency. People ask if coaches toss and turn, unable to sleep, and the answer is: you bet! I tossed and turned thinking about roster choices all the time. But usually by the night before a game, I'd have done most of my work and would be looking forward to the action. I loved taking the sideline and having the best view of the action. That was the fun part. I could see everything from there, and after so many years, I'd noticed that time slows down for me during the game. I would see plays unfold as if in slow motion. Who wouldn't enjoy that? That was a fun game to watch, and it was both a boost and a reminder of how far we still had to go to qualify for the World Cup. Clint cast aside any remaining concerns about his health and had an explosive game, recording his second career hat trick, and we cruised to a 6–0 win, led by Christian's dynamic playmaking. Instead of last place in qualifying, we'd moved up to fourth. "This team is really strong mentally, and to come back from two losses was really impressive," Christian said afterward. "It showed good heart."

Four days later we would face Panama at Estadio Rommel Fernández in the capital. Again, Christian and Clint were key players for us. Clint, in only his second game back with the national team after missing time with the heart issue, took a pass from Christian early in the second half to score his fifty-sixth goal for the national team, putting him one behind Landon Donovan for the all-time record. Panama answered, and the game was as rough and tumble as you expect when going to Central America for a World Cup qualifying game. We held on, and I was proud of the team.

"In an emphatic destruction of Honduras on Friday, the United States men's soccer team seemed to glide effortlessly across the field in almost dreamlike fashion, producing six goals and three critical points that moved them closer to their goal of qualifying for the 2018 World Cup," David Waldstein wrote in the *New York Times*. "A steamy, humid night at Estadio Rommel Fernández four days later turned out to be much more of a slog. Facing 90-degree heat at kickoff and thousands of passionate fans throughout, the Americans managed only one goal against Panama in Tuesday's qualifier, but it was enough to secure them a point—never an easy thing to come by on the road in the CONCACAF region."

There were so many ways the game could have unraveled. It took a terrific effort to avoid that. We showed some mental strength in Panama City on a day when we could have folded up the tent after we conceded a goal right before the half. We were dealing with difficult conditions, a field that was a mess and the usual dubious officiating, and the guys showed a lot of character and experience. We walked out of there with a point on a day when a lot of other teams would not have. I'd love to see what it would be like if some of these European teams were asked to get a result under those conditions. I think people might be surprised. I was happy for Clint, seeing him return to form for us in such a spectacular way. For him it was first and foremost about the team, but it was also partly personal.

"When I was able to come back and start playing again with Seattle, I really appreciated Bruce calling me in so quick to be a part of things with the national team," Clint says now. "I wanted to pay him back, and I felt like I was able to do that in my first two games back with four goals in two games."

I flew back to LA on a commercial flight after that game, because the team charter was flying to Miami, and I ended up sitting next to Clint. I'm not sure he and I had ever talked more than ten minutes at a stretch in all the years I'd known him, but we talked for about three hours on that flight. It was very enjoyable, just a relaxed, wide-ranging talk more about life in general than anything to do with soccer. The talk reinforced what I'd been thinking about Clint, which was that he was in a good place.

We talked about his family life in Seattle. Clint grew up Catholic, and his faith is important to him. He and his wife, Bethany, have two sons and two daughters. On that flight, he was telling me that they have the kids enrolled in Catholic school in Seattle and they can walk them to school every day. He was very positive. He was happy with the Sounders. He was really in a happy, comfortable place in his life and thrilled to be back with the national team.

That was a different Clint on that flight than the one I'd known in the past. Before he went through his issues with his heart, I really don't think Clint would have been able to have a three-hour conversation like that. He'd always been a guy who kept everything to himself, so it was interesting hearing him open up on the value he placed on his family, and he knew how important family was to me as well. The fact that he could really appreciate and respect the career he'd had, and also realize how fortunate he was that it hadn't been cut short after the health concerns—that was a plus for him, and it made me think he'd be able to retire gracefully when his time came. He always had the right perspective on things, and I knew he was a good leader. In the past, guys would say that Clint cared but he was kind of on his own, but by that phase of his career, he was much more involved with the other players.

I remember one time when I was with the Galaxy and Clint was playing in Fulham, where he scored fifty goals from 2007 to 2012. We were looking at a Fulham goalkeeper for the Galaxy, so I called him up to see what he thought of that player. I'll say this: he was honest.

"I don't know much about the guy," Clint said.

"Don't you practice with him every day?" I asked, wanting to laugh.

"Yeah," he said. "I just never really thought about it."

"Clint, he's a goalkeeper," I said.

"Yeah, but I don't pay that much attention."

That was typical Clint. He was in his own world at that time, but he'd grown up since then. It made me glad to connect with a key player like that, because I knew there would always be ups and downs.

A Fresh Start

Going into our two World Cup qualifying matches in June 2017, I was concerned about our eighteen-year-old star, Christian Pulisic, coming off his first full season in the Budesliga. I'd visited Christian's club team in Germany on May 3. Three days later he played in a match against Hoffenheim, then another one on May 13 and finally on May 20. Dortmund wrapped up the season with a 4–3 win over Bremen after Christian earned a penalty to set up the game-winning goal. Then in the final of the DFB-Pokal (the German Soccer Association Cup) on May 27, Christian played the second half and again Dortmund won on a penalty kick after a foul on Christian. It was all great experience for a young player, and the pictures of Christian holding the cup in the air made me smile. But it was also a lot of minutes of high-level competition to cap Christian's first year of elite-level soccer. I knew he was bone-tired after all that, and we'd have to watch him closely in our two June qualifiers, against Trinidad and Tobago in Denver on June 8 and then in Mexico City against Mexico on June 11, two matches at high altitude, played just three days apart.

Because of our losses the year before, we went into the Trinidad game knowing we had to win. When you start the Hex the way we started, your home games are must wins. However, we needed a strategy for game two as well, also to be played in the thinner air far above sea level.

International football has changed so much. It used to be that when you played a small country like Trinidad, you might have to think about one or two quality players, but the team in general would be lacking in international experience. In the past Trinidad had Dwight Yorke, who played so well for Aston Villa and Manchester United in the 1990s, and teams had to focus only on him. Now you go into these games facing a number of experienced players. Part of that is the rise of Major League Soccer, where many of Trinidad's top players are now on teams. It's the same with Panama, Honduras, Costa Rica—more players are getting experience around the world. You go against Costa Rica, you face Keylor Navas, who just happens to be the starting goalkeeper for Real Madrid, one of the best club teams in history.

Every game is a tough game now.

On May 29, when Christian arrived in camp before our friendly game with Venezuela, it was clear he was showing the physical wear and tear of a tightly contested Bundesliga season. We gave him a day off before he started training with the team. The day after he arrived, news broke that his manager at Dortmund, Thomas Tuchel, was moving on. I was a little surprised by the news. I'd hit it off with Tuchel and found him smart and knowledgeable. He was being given his marching orders despite arguably a very successful season. The club CEO complained that he and the sporting director had "worn ourselves out during this time in our workings with the coaching team." It was another reminder of how critically important good and consistent communication is for the success of any manager. Without that, problems always develop, sooner or later.

For Christian, the change would probably work out well. He wasn't as taken as I was by Tuchel and was happy to make the most of the situation with whomever came next. When Christian found out that the new coach would be the former Dutch midfielder Peter Bosz, who was the manager at Ajax Amsterdam, he was excited by what he saw as Bosz's "attack-minded" approach.

John Brooks was also going through change in his Bundesliga career. We talked at breakfast on the morning of May 30, the day it was going to be announced that he was completing a transfer from Hertha Berlin to Wolfsburg for approximately 20 million euros. Some would question this move, because Wolfsburg had had to survive a playoff battle to remain in the Bundesliga. This wasn't even a lateral move, which was odd. Typically, a player in John's position would love to move on to a bigger club or league. But every player has to know what's best for himself, and John made clear to me he was very happy about the move. He felt strongly that he would be in a position to grow and develop at Wolfsburg, a club heavily investing in improving its status in the league. I was glad to hear it and left breakfast thinking that a happy John Brooks was a great thing.

Geoff Cameron was the only one to surprise me. The last camp we had him in, for Honduras and Panama, he had complained the whole week about something. He wasn't right; you could see it the day before the first game, but we went with him, and he had to come out in the fifty-eighth minute against Honduras. Ten minutes later, Brooks had to come out, so we'd burned two substitutions. Thank God it was 6–0 at the time. Then we thought Geoff would be starting against Panama, but the day before, he said, "I can't go." His knee was hurting when he arrived in camp before Trinidad and Mexico, so we really didn't know what to think.

"You know, I can't afford to take you out," I told him before the Trinidad game. "Are you ready to go?"

He said he was. And he played a good ninety minutes for us.

I decided we'd go with Clint and Jozy up front against Trinidad, leaving Bobby Wood mostly out of the action for that game, and then he'd be fresh against Mexico and we could take advantage of his speed. Bobby wasn't happy about this decision at all. That's fine. That's good, even. You want guys who are burning to play. If they're a little pissed off about not getting a shot, that's good to see. But they also have to keep their emotions in check and keep their own role in perspective. Bobby was having trouble doing that.

Trinidad was the game we had to have—a tie would have been a disaster for us. When the game started, I was not very happy. Trinidad was not very good in terms of attacking, but their defensive organization was excellent. Our passing wasn't sharp enough. We needed Clint to be a little bit more active. It was another of those times when we seemed like a new team, thrown together for the first time. We brought Fabian Johnson into the lineup, along with Darlington Nagbe, and in practice we made a big point of getting the right spacing. We knew Trinidad was going to drop back and defend with eight players behind the ball, so we had to space ourselves properly. Early in the game we kept falling short, but as time went on, we started getting the spacing right and creating some chances from wide positions.

At halftime I just told them spacing had to be better and we had to move the ball a little bit quicker and get guys in front of the goal. We got the quick ball movement I wanted on the first goal, which was a collective effort featuring both younger and more experienced players:

It started with our captain, Michael Bradley, pressuring the ball until DeAndre Yedlin won the ball and played it into Nagbe. He beat a player and combined with Dempsey for a one-two around the penalty area, with Yedlin using his speed to join the attack down the right flank. Nagbe touched the ball to Yedlin, who put it across the six-yard box to Pulisic, who slid feetfirst to finish off a great goal. Michael started the second goal as well, standing up their striker. Geoff Cameron retrieved the ball and passed to Pulisic in the middle third of the field. Pulisic then passed off to Yedlin, overlapping down the right flank, then to Altidore, and Pulisic received the ball and beat the keeper to the near post for his second goal of the match. Fatigue set in for Trinidad at that point. The second goal came at the sixty-first minute, and that's around when you see teams at high altitudes starting to feel it. From there on, it was just two tired teams struggling to stay sharp, and we held on for the 2–0 win. That was no laugher. Trinidad had improved greatly. They gave us a tough game, but we played well enough in the second half to get our three points. Mission accomplished.

Christian was interviewed on TV just after the game and did great. He struck just the kind of confident chord we like to see heading into Azteca Stadium days later facing the huge challenge of going against Mexico.

"It's going to be a tough one down there, in Mexico especially, but we really want some revenge on them for when they got us earlier this year," Christian said. "So we're really confident going into that game, and we're going to come out with a win there, too."

The words were delivered in a modest, almost shy tone, his voice trailing off at the end, but of course he made some headlines. Like this one: "Pulisic: 'The United States Is Going to Beat Mexico.'"

There was talk later that his quotes—and the headlines—fired up the Mexicans. No question it fired up the Mexican press to ask some questions and stir things up. I loved it all. I wanted to beat Mexico too, and I don't want players on my team who don't think we're about to beat the tough opponent we're going against. Did that rile up the Mexicans? I have no idea. I didn't ask them, and I couldn't care less what they thought. We went into that game in Mexico believing we were going to get a result. We never thought about losing or falling back on some excuses about how the circumstances were such that we'd give a good effort but walk off the field with nothing and that would be OK. No way. Not for one second. We had the mind-set that we would be walking off the field with something.

Azteca

Knowing how hard it is to play two World Cup qualifying games at high altitude within three days, we did everything we could to make the guys comfortable. We didn't fly coach or commercial. We chartered a specially outfitted seventy-seat 757, the same plane a lot of NBA teams use. For the flight down to Mexico that Friday, we had it totally full. Up front were the players, who had sleeper beds, and in one of the rear sections we decided to bring along some sponsors, some media, and our board of directors, including Sunil Gulati, the president of the United States Soccer Federation, and Carlos Cordeiro, the vice president. Once we arrived in Mexico City, I was introduced to our board members, including Donna Shalala, who was Secretary of Health and Human Services in the Clinton administration and went on to serve as president of the University of Miami before retiring. I told her we had someone in common.

"I know Jim Larrañaga, who is your basketball coach at Miami," I told her. "We coached together at Virginia."

She loved it. She pulled out her phone and started texting Jim. She also mentioned that at age seventy-six, she was still teaching.

"Really?" I said. "Graduates, I guess?"

"No, undergraduates," she said.

I actually spent a chunk of that flight looking at tape, which generally I don't care to do. Usually my coaching staff handles all the editing. But this was a special case. I remember how different the technology was during my first run with the national team and what it was like editing tape to show the team. It took forever. In those days there was no such thing as digital. To make edits you had to run through the entire ninety minutes of the game again. We'd spend twenty-four hours working on an Apple computer waiting for the analog system to produce our edits for scouting. If you edited three games, you'd have to run through all three games, and the software we used would pick out the edits you marked and pull them out. Now technology has come so far: it's all digital, and edited videos are produced in a fraction of the time.

We cleared customs in Mexico City in nothing flat, literally just a few minutes. That's one of the great things about flying charters and having a first-class administrative staff, led by Tom King and Jon Fleishman. Then we climbed onto the team bus for the ride over to our hotel, the Four Seasons, a beautiful facility along Mexico City's Paseo de la Reforma. At dinner I got up to speak to the players and went over what we'd been saying for days, that we needed to change the lineup as one way to fight fatigue. Because of Mexico's participation in the Confederations Cup, we'd agreed to an unheard-of schedule, playing Mexico on two days' rest, and we were playing at 7,200 feet.

"We've got to make some changes," I told the team, reviewing our predicament.

Something felt off. I didn't like it. I'm not saying anyone said anything to indicate actual uneasiness with our plan, but the lack of unanimous conviction was obvious. Our team psychologist, Tom Perrin, agreed with me that there was some work to be done.

"You should talk to a couple guys," he told me.

A couple guys? That got me thinking. I'd known I wanted to talk to Clint and Jozy and a couple others, but my gut was telling me more was necessary, so I listened to my gut. I decided to have a one-on-one meeting with every single player. I wanted to hear from them directly and make no mistake about where they were, heading into this game. All those meetings would take some time and take away from some of my game preparation, but that's why I had assembled an excellent coaching staff. Every player is different, and those differences have to be honored and embraced and, above all, understood.

We had very few rules for our players. The most important rule was to be on time and be respectful. We didn't give them a curfew. I said to myself, *I'm not sitting in a hotel lobby waiting to see who's coming in late at night.* We had breakfast and lunch together at the hotel, but only a few team dinners. Mostly I left them on their own. It was good for them. They built a bond among themselves. I didn't tell them where to go or what to do. I didn't give them a hint as to when I thought they were supposed to get in or any of that. I trusted them to be responsible, and they were.

That Saturday morning after the guys ate breakfast, anytime between eight and eleven, they'd come in to see me one by one. None of this was announced earlier. My assistant, Martha Romero, informed them one by one to come see me. As each one left, I'd write a little note to myself.

Darlington Nagbe came in first and admitted he was a little tired, which was great. We always want to hear the truth. We had him down as a reserve.

"You'll probably play thirty minutes," I told him, and that was what he ended up playing.

I'd told goalkeeper Brad Guzan weeks in advance that I would probably play him against Mexico. He hadn't been with us for the games against Honduras and Panama because his wife, Breanne, was due to have their second baby. They were still living in England at that time, before he came back to the US to play for Atlanta United. I told him, "You've got to be there with your wife. It's a foreign country, some things will be different." So when I saw him at our next camp, I told him right away to be ready to play against Mexico, and he was.

Dax McCarty was one of the guys I thought would play, but I wasn't sure, and I had to tell him that. "I don't know," I said. "I'm going to talk to Michael. If he can go, then he's going to go. He's the captain of our team."

Dax said he understood the situation and he'd be ready to play. We've been through a lot of stuff with him in our camps.

Fabian was tired too. He had played sixty-five minutes against Trinidad and struggled a little physically. He'd missed about eight weeks from the Gladbach team schedule; he wasn't fully fit, and the altitude was hard on him.

Michael Bradley came in next. "I can play," he said.

"Are you sure?" I asked him. "Do you feel . . . ?"

"Yeah," he said.

He didn't even let me finish the question. It didn't matter what I asked him, the answer was going to be "Yeah." He was playing.

"The choice is, you play with Kellyn or Dax, and I'm thinking it will probably be Kellyn."

"I'm fine with that," Michael said.

So I put it down in my notes: "Playing with Acosta."

When Christian came in, I looked him in the eye, as I did all the guys, and saw he wasn't eager to have much of a conversation. He's not real talkative, which is fine. He's still a young kid.

"You're gonna play unless you tell me otherwise," I said, raising my eyebrows a little.

"No, I definitely want to play," he said.

"How do you feel? You think you can go ninety?"

He was straight with me. "If I have to defend a lot, it's going to be challenging," he said.

This would be his third game in a row playing ninety minutes at altitude: Venezuela in Salt Lake City, a friendly, then Trinidad in Denver, and Mexico in Mexico City. He would be working at both ends, and I knew fatigue was going to bite especially hard for him.

Clint Dempsey came in next. It was our third conversation since I'd subbed him out of the Trinidad game after the sixty-minute mark and he boiled over a little. Clint was not happy and demonstrated his displeasure with the change. That's just Clint. He's fiery and proud.

"For me it was important for him to have a one-on-one talk with me and kind of understand my frustrations and figure out where I was coming from, and I could figure out where he was coming from, so there was no gray area," he said.

Matt Hedges was down on my list to start, but I wasn't sure about him, either. I laid it out straight. "I think you're going to start the game. But I'm not sure yet. Wait until I talk to all the other guys."

When Kellyn Acosta came in, I could have told him he was going to play for sure, but since I was meeting with every player, I wanted to look at these guys and form my impressions. I told him it was Dax or him getting the nod, but I didn't know yet.

Geoff Cameron might have been the only one to surprise me. Given the fact that he needed to come out of the Honduras game in March and the fact that he had been dealing with a number of injuries, I doubted that he'd be able to play two games in four days for us.

But Geoff wanted to play. "I've got more than fifty caps," he told me when he came in for his one-on-one meeting. "I never come out."

His response surprised me, but this was clearly a guy we wanted on the field. "I'm ready to go," he said. He'd made his point.

Geoff is a good player, so if he wanted to play and gave me his assurances that he was fit and healthy enough, then he was in the mix. That left Hedges out.

John Brooks came in next, and we both knew he was going to be a reserve, but it was a good meeting.

"We're planning on playing a back three," I told him. John doesn't like playing in that alignment, with three defenders working together on the backline. He just doesn't feel comfortable, not having played much in that formation. I'd always had him down for a reserve role in the Mexico game, but we knew we had work to do to get him ready to play in a back three down the road if that was the formation that made sense for us.

John was in a good frame of mind. He was pretty pleased with himself, having played well against Trinidad, other than perhaps one lapse of concentration that almost led to a goal.

"You're a six-foot-five center back," I told him. "You should not be getting beat in the air in the box."

That was part of his learning process. We wanted him to be an important part of our team moving forward, but we were all getting to know each other still, like starting over with a new team, and it was going to take time.

Bobby Wood was ready to play but still needed calming down. For days he had not been able to get over the fact that he didn't start against Trinidad.

"Time to move on, Bobby," I told him.

"Yeah, but I thought I'd be in there," he said.

"Doesn't matter what you thought before, Bobby. Forget it! You played ten minutes against Trinidad. You played well. You did your job. You can't take that back. It's done. We're moving forward."

Even in Azteca Stadium, the day before the game, Wood was still moping around, fixated.

"Bobby!" I said. "It's over with! You're starting against Mexico."

That wasn't enough to break the spell he'd cast on himself.

"And if we get a penalty, you're taking it!"

He still didn't say anything.

"Are you good with that?" I asked him. "Or should I give it to somebody else?"

When I asked him that, an amazing thing happened. Bobby smiled for the first time. I'd reached him. He'd finally moved on.

You've got to get to know your guys. They all have their quirks, and they all have off days. You've got twenty-three players, and you've got to handle them twenty-three different ways. Human nature can push a coach to treat some guys as if they're interchangeable. I try never to do that. Bad things happen when you forget that your players are people and they have issues like anyone else. You need to respect their individuality.

I told Graham Zusi he might or might not start, depending on what I heard from DeAndre Yedlin. DeAndre came in next and told me was fine. He was very fit and had a huge tank—he could run all day. He had really grown as a player since going to Newcastle in 2016, improving both technically and tactically. He was very gifted physically, extremely fast, quick, and strong. Nobody should get by him. As a younger player in Seattle, he was highly dependent on his speed. He played with the attitude, *If I get beat, I'm fast enough to recover.* That's not good enough. I remember Landon Donovan beating him in a playoff game when I coached him with the Galaxy and scoring a important goal. Landon just outthought him.

"A player should never get behind you," I had told DeAndre at the time. Now, though, he protected the space behind him and those kind of plays seldom happened anymore.

Tim Howard was next. There's not a player whom I have more respect for. He's been a great soldier for US soccer. However, I felt that playing him against Mexico would be pushing him on the physical end, and the plan was to go with Brad Guzan. Tim wanted to play. He let our goalkeeper coach, Matt Reis, know how he felt, so I thought Tim and I have might have a little bit of a debate, but he'd moved on and was all about the team.

"I'm OK," he said. "I support everything. I'll be with Brad."

One factor in our decision making was Tim's continuing recovery from a groin injury requiring surgery that he'd sustained in our World Cup qualifier against Mexico in November 2016. I knew he'd have loved to be in there at Azteca and get revenge for that loss, but the game would have been physically challenging for him, and I anticipated that this game would require a lot of kicking from our goalkeeper. Brad's kicking game would be a real positive for us.

I finished all the one-on-one meetings, and then we gathered for a team meeting at one o'clock, which went well because they all knew where they were. No open questions were festering. The guys were relaxed and fired up. It was a far cry from the meeting the night before, which had left me with an uneasy feeling. Then we went over to Azteca and trained and that night had another team meeting. They were ready to go.

Every coach does things differently. There's no one right way. We had two mottos for the guys as they came into camp. One was "Every player in this camp belongs here," and the other was "Your club shirt weighs the same as the national team shirt. Relax and show who you are." This was a team that had been starved for direction, so it was worth going all out to make sure we were all on the same page.

Alejandro Bedoya was one player I'd been absolutely impressed with as I got to know him in our camps since taking over the US team again. Both his father and grandfather had played professional soccer in Colombia, but Alejandro was born in Englewood, New Jersey, and grew up in a town outside of Fort

Lauderdale, Florida. He played two years at Fairleigh Dickinson and two at Boston College before going over to Europe to start his professional career, then coming back to the MLS to play for the Philadelphia Union. The more I talked to him, the more I liked what I saw. The first time I got to work with him was at our camp in January 2017; I found him to be a really good player and also really bright. On most days, though, he's just outside our starting eleven, like a sixth man in basketball.

"Your role is probably to be a reserve for the most part, and you've got to understand your role," I told him.

I was asking a player who had been around and earned respect to take a reduced role, and he was accepting that all the way without blinking an eye. When guys put the team first and accept a new role, that's something all the other players notice and respect. It becomes contagious.

Tim Howard could not have been a better teammate leading up to the Mexico game. I'm sure it was hard for him to swallow not getting a shot at playing in Mexico. He's an intense competitor, but he understood our thinking and he accepted it. He was there for Brad in every way he could be. In training the day before the game, he was working with Brad, going over things together, supporting him and encouraging him, and on game day he was terrific as well. You saw him respond to the moment in such an amazing way and you thought, *We're building a team.*

There were articles in the press noting that the game was even bigger than usual, because at the time the US president was Donald Trump, whose talk of building a wall on the border with Mexico inflamed a lot of emotion, but a soccer match is a soccer match, not a debate over politics. As Tim Howard put it, "When these guys are bearing down on you, Donald Trump is the last thing on your mind."

It's an amazing feeling to walk out onto the field at Azteca to play Mexico. The spectators are right on top of you, and of course it's very loud, but something about the acoustics makes it feel as if they're all shouting directly into your ear. It's basically impossible for a coach to communicate with the players. Besides dealing with the thin air at 7,200 feet, they were on their own.

My first visit to Azteca was at the 1986 World Cup, twenty years after it first opened. I attended the quarter-final, semifinal, and final game in that storied stadium, which in those days held 120,000 spectators. I witnessed Diego Maradona's illegal "Hand of God" goal against England, which the referee failed to nullify, as well as the other goal he scored that day, the "goal of the century," considered one of the best ever tallied in the sport—and Argentina's ultimate World Cup victory. Over the years, a number of remodeling projects have reduced the capacity to just under 90,000, but it's an intensely challenging place to play, intimidating and at the same time a beautiful celebration of our game. It also offers a tremendous home-field advantage for the Mexican team, which has had an incredible winning percentage at Azteca.

As the coach, you can't really let yourself get too excited about anything that happens early in a game. You want to stay dialed in and alert to everything that's happening on the field, and you can't afford to lose your concentration for even a moment or two. From the start, I was happy to see Michael Bradley getting after the ball. Six minutes into the game, he intercepted a pass from Javier "Chicharito" Hernández in the center circle and instantly pushed the ball forward, eluding three defenders who were slow to react. Michael surged into the open space, and chipped a shot on goal from long range that floated right in under the crossbar. He became only the sixth American ever to score at Estadia Azteca, and it was a beautiful goal. I wasn't going to celebrate anything just yet, but I was smiling from ear to ear on the sideline. Grant Wahl, *Sports Illustrated*'s veteran soccer writer, not usually one to gush, dubbed it a "wondergoal," and it was hard to argue with that.

We didn't think this was any kind of fluke, taking a lead over Mexico at Azteca. We were in the game to win it. Even after Carlos Vela scored in the twenty-third minute to tie it up, we were very much thinking in terms of finding a way to win. Mexico's goal was disappointing. DaMarcus Beasley pushed Vela in toward the middle of the field, and our players were late to step to him, giving him room to get off a quick shot. At 1–1 the game was on.

At the eighty-sixth minute, Christian had a great chance, but you could see that fatigue had clearly set in, and his effort was off goal. In the end, we couldn't put them away, but our strong defensive effort enabled us to walk off the field with a huge point. That point moved our team into third place in the Hex.

Gold Cup 2017

I've always believed that you win by winning. The more you win, the more the players learn *how* to win, even on a bad day when everything goes wrong. The more wins they experience, the deeper the commitment they make to doing all that's required to have a winning team.

We wanted to win the 2017 Gold Cup, a tournament featuring teams from North America, Central America, and the Caribbean, to send a message that the United States was back after a disappointing fourth-place showing in the previous Gold Cup in 2015. Compared to the goal of qualifying for the World Cup, the Gold Cup was far less important, but we approached it with a sense of high purpose. We wanted to develop young players and get a look at some new faces to see how they would fare in challenging international competition. Balancing those two priorities was a juggling act, like so much of what you do as a coach. The trick was to think through what you wanted to do, make a plan and stick with it—which was just what we did.

Almost as much as any goal scored, the story of our 2017 Gold Cup could be summed up by the shot shown on the TV broadcast of our third game, a shot of a luxury box at FirstEnergy Stadium in Cleveland, home of the NFL Browns. We'd tied Panama 1–1, edged Martinique 3–2, and were in a scoreless tie in the first half against Nicaragua when the camera panned over to the box and a close-up of Michael Bradley and Tim Howard in US team jackets, watching the game. Our plan for the tournament was to use the first three games of the Gold Cup to look at new players, then bring in the cavalry once we got to the knockout stage. That would have included Christian Pulisic as well, but because he had a new coach to get to know at Dortmund, he wasn't available. Michael, our team captain, and Tim, our best player in the last World Cup, were the cavalry, or that at least was the story line for the TV viewers at home, who probably assumed this was some last-minute decision on my part and loved the drama of it. We were going for a win in the Gold Cup—that was the message.

The qualifying round had given some fresh faces a chance to shine, especially our twenty-two-year-old striker Jordan Morris. He grew up in Washington state and joined the development of the Seattle Sounders, where his father worked as chief medical director, then went to Stanford and in his junior year and led the Cardinals to an NCAA championship, scoring five of Stanford's twelve goals in the tournament. Jordan is a great kid. He's very bright and could do something else in his life and be successful. He didn't need to play soccer. But he was alert and incredibly athletic and got better week to week and game to game, which was really encouraging to see.

Our first game, against Panama, was our weakest. It was actually the first time the US failed to win its opening game in the Gold Cup, for people who pay attention to those kinds of things. We scored first on a goal from Dom Dwyer, who was born in England and plays in the MLS for Orlando. It was Dom's second straight game with a goal, counting a friendly with Ghana, but it didn't hold up. Ten minutes later, Gabriel Torres beat Brad Guzan and we ended up having to settle for a 1–1 tie.

"We didn't play well on the day," I said matter-of-factly afterward. "We didn't deal well with their pressure."

Four days later in Tampa, we rode an Omar Gonzalez goal and two from Jordan Morris in the win over Martinique. Our goals in the 3–0 win over Nicaragua to close out the qualifying round came from Joe Corona, Kelyn Rowe, and Matt Miazga, showing we could mix it up. Finally we were through to the elimination round, and we were able to add the more experienced players we'd always been planning to add after the group stage: Clint Dempsey, Jozy Altidore, Michael Bradley, and Tim Howard, who all started in our next game, against El Salvador, as well as Darlington Nagbe.

The whole charge-of-the-cavalry angle on our run through the Gold Cup looked good on TV, but I knew it might take time to add so many players and have the chemistry work. I was right to have concerns. In the first half against El Salvador, playing before 31,615 at Lincoln Financial Field in Philadelphia, we did not look like a team out there. We were sloppy and couldn't find a rhythm. El Salvador's game plan was to foul, foul, foul, and there would be forty-five fouls in the game by the end. With players falling on the ground all over the place, we had to be good to get anything going—and for the first half hour, we were not good. Finally we came together to press the attack late in the first half, and Omar Gonzalez and Eric Lichaj each scored to give us a 2–0 lead, which held up.

In the second half, it really started getting ugly out there. I thought I was watching Mike Tyson going against Evander Holyfield. Here's how *Sports Illustrated* captured the scene: "Things got a little weird for Jozy Altidore Wednesday night. O.K., they got a lot weird. Altidore was bitten and had a nipple tweaked. . . . In a bizarre sequence inside the El Salvador box at around the hour mark of the 2–0 USA win, defender Henry Romero got a little handsy and followed up by doing his best Luis Suárez impression in trying to agitate Altidore."

Jozy had the perfect reply after the game.

"My girl is mad at me," he said. "She's mad at me, she's mad at Romero. She's like, 'Only I can bite you, only I can grab your nipples.'"

In case anyone thought Romero had just lost his mind, incredibly enough, another player also resorted to biting: Darwin Cerén chomped at Omar Gonzalez's shoulder in a sequence that was captured vividly on tape, just like Romero's antics with Jozy. You have to wonder: Don't they realize this stuff is going to be recorded forever? And as to officiating, if I'm the referee for a game in which two players on one side bite players on the other, I'd see that as being on me. One guy, OK. Two? How do you not crack down on that? And yet neither bite resulted in the slightest consequence during the game itself. After the fact, CONCACAF announced that Romero was being suspended for El Salvador's next six games for biting Jozy, and Cerén was suspended for three games for more of what they called "anti-sporting behavior." I'm not sure those suspensions are much of a deterrent to others taking that road.

Next up was Costa Rica, the team that had inflicted that 4–0 pummeling on the US team in the last game before I took over again. This was a well-coached team that knew how to maintain discipline at the defensive end. We came out playing a lot better than we had against El Salvador and pushed the attack. For the first half, we had the ball 61 percent of the time to 39 percent for the Ticos, but we couldn't break through, and at halftime it was 0–0. I'd spoken with Clint Dempsey again and again about using him in different ways, and by that point in his career, I liked the idea of bringing him off the bench in the second half to provide a jolt of energy.

"I was cool with it," Clint says now. "The way I look at it, man, in an ideal world, this is if you could control things, if you're going to only play sixty minutes and come off, or you had the choice to come on and play thirty minutes, I'd rather come on and play thirty minutes and kind of go after teams when they're tired and make an impact. I'm thirty-four now. To think that I'm going to start and play every game is a little bit far-fetched, so I just want to have the impact that will help the team. If that's my role, then I'm happy to play it."

Clint had a hungry look when I subbed him in for Paul Arriola at the sixty-sixth minute of the Costa Rica game. He wanted a goal to tie Landon Donovan for the all-time lead with fifty-seven, but mostly he wanted to make something happen. Six minutes after he came into the game, Clint flicked the ball back with his right foot, surprising the Costa Rica defenders to clear a little room, then pushed the ball up and sent a perfect pass to Jozy Altidore, splitting two defenders; Jozy scored to make it 1–0. Then came another chance. Clint lined up to take a free kick from about twenty-five yards out and hooked his low shot around the wall to find the corner. We were up 2–0 and Clint had made history.

"It's a fabulous record for any player to have," I said afterward. "It was something that was important to Clint. And to score that goal in a big game, I'm sure makes it even more special."

Everyone assumed we would play our rivals Mexico in the Gold Cup final, but Jamaica gave them a tough game in the other semifinal and made it through. My first professional game at MLS was at Spartan Stadium. My first game with the national team was at Spartan Stadium. We had rekindled the US national program in San Jose four months earlier when we beat Honduras, and now we were looking to win a Gold Cup nearby in Santa Clara at Levi's Stadium, the 49ers' home.

Players are going to make mistakes. You hope they don't make bad mistakes in a high-profile game like a Gold Cup final, but if they do, you look to see how they respond. Jordan Morris blew his assignment on a corner kick in the fiftieth minute, by loosely marking his man, Je-Vaughn Watson, who converted to tie it up

1–1, costing us the lead we'd built on Jozy Altidore's twenty-eight-yard free kick in the forty-fifth minute. Jordan was hard on himself and played even harder, looking for a chance to redeem himself. It came in the eighty-eighth minute on an opportunistic shot from fourteen yards out after the Jamaica defense tried to clear a cross from Gyasi Zardes and failed. That was three goals in the tournament for Jordan, tying him with Canada's Alphonso Davies for the tournament lead.

"I was nervous," Jordan said afterward. "It was my guy that scored on the goal, so I was trying to make up for it any way that I could. Obviously, I take responsibility for that. But luckily I could put one in the back of the net."

Winning feels great. We weren't building the Gold Cup victory up as more than it was, but we'd found out a lot about ourselves along the way and taken some important strides forward. I'd looked to instill more confidence and more joy in playing in the team, and that was something that came through in the Gold Cup final. It was also a celebration of a team that reflected the patchwork-quilt diversity of the United States, starting with the Italian American coach.

Even the *New Yorker* took notice, running a story by Clint Smith under the headline "A Joyfully Defiant US Men's National Team Takes the Gold Cup."

Altidore, whose parents came to the United States from Haiti, is one of many sons of immigrants on the US team. There's Omar Gonzalez, whose parents are from Mexico; Matt Miazga, the son of Polish immigrants; Darlington Nagbe, born in Liberia; and Juan Agudelo, who was born in Colombia. Watching them celebrate, I thought of the kids I had seen the day before playing soccer at a park near my home, in Washington, D.C. Their foreheads glistened in the afternoon sun, their brown bodies moved with the rau-

cous howl of their adolescent voices. With the promise of that pluralism seemingly under siege as of late, the rejoicing of the men's team felt almost defiant. . . .

There are tough World Cup qualifying matches to come: the team must win a slate of contests to secure a trip to an eighth consecutive World Cup, in Russia, in 2018. For one evening, though, regardless of the larger significance—or insignificance—of the Gold Cup, we could celebrate a team that looks like the country we are quickly becoming, and perhaps the country we have always been.

A Nightmare

I felt good going into our World Cup qualifying game against Costa Rica at Red Bull Arena in New Jersey on September 1, 2017. The team had momentum after winning the Gold Cup, though injuries to our backline had me concerned, too. As an experienced coach, you can never stop thinking about nightmare scenarios. We'd gone from last place with zero points in the Hex to third. We were on track to qualify for the World Cup, with only four games more to go in the Hex, but if we fell short, I'd have to live through my worst nightmare.

Whenever I'd been asked, I'd maintained that qualifying for the 2018 World Cup was going to be extremely challenging. Every qualifying campaign has its ups and downs, its ebb and flow. That's all a part of the exercise. You're always going to have injuries, but it did hurt to lose both John Brooks and DeAndre Yedlin, for both were considered starters in our backline. With them gone, it was hard to create consistency in our backline and first eleven.

Preparing the roster for Costa Rica and Honduras was difficult. For the Gold Cup, I left a majority of European-based players with their club teams, but now I had to plan for their participation in these upcoming World Cup qualifying games. I couldn't help but feel that by adding Christian Pulisic, Geoff Cameron, Bobby Wood, Tim Ream, Fabian Johnson, and others to our roster, we would have a stronger team. However, I had some reservations. These players were just entering their club seasons and were not fully match fit. In addition, it was never going to be easy bringing in players who had been away from the team for an extended period. Logic would tell you that Geoff Cameron and Bobby Wood and naturally Pulisic were perfect choices. There would be some questions raised about Ream and Johnson, but my thinking was that if we were going to use these players, we had to do so in game one, when the conditions would be much more suitable for European-based players—less heat and humidity and a home field. The game in Harrison, New Jersey, versus Costa Rica was going to be played in mild conditions, 70 degrees, good field, and, we hoped, an enthusiastic home crowd. The game in San Pedro Sula, Honduras, was going to be played in very hot and humid conditions on a less than perfect field in a hostile environment.

Most of our players reported to camp on Sunday, August 28, after playing their weekend games, and seven other players reported on Monday. It would take us until Wednesday to have all the players close to being fully recovered from their weekend games and ready to train at full speed. With the Costa Rica game scheduled for Friday, September 1, we were operating in a small window and had little time to fully prepare the team. That made selecting the team more difficult. Our starting eleven would include five European-based players: Geoff Cameron, Tim Ream, Fabian Johnson, Chris Pulisic, and Bobby Wood. Our 4-4-2 formation would be finalized with Tim Howard, Graham Zusi, Jorge Villafaña, Michael Bradley, Darlington Nagbe, and Jozy Altidore. This would be our third game versus Costa Rica in the past ten months. We knew their personnel and their tactics very well by now. We figured that they would defend with numbers behind the ball and rely on good team shape and organization, counterattacking via Bryan Ruiz and Marco Ureña, and the goal-keeping of Real Madrid's Keylor Navas. They would be pleased to leave the United States with one point, so we needed to be sharp on both ends of the field. We would have to play well, not concede a goal, and be opportunistic if we got chances to score. There would be no margin for error.

The game started at a good pace, with Costa Rica surprisingly pressing higher up the field. After fifteen minutes, we established a decent rhythm yet failed to deliver. We looked ready to take the lead at the twenty-six-minute mark, when Graham Zusi played the ball from midfield down the right side to Christian Pulisic, but he was swarmed with defenders every time he touched the ball. Christian took one touch, behind the Costa Rican backline, and before Bryan Oviedo and Francisco Calvo could close him down, he delivered the ball in front of the goal to an on-charging Jozy Altidore, ten yards out, who was taken down by Kendall Watson. Nothing subtle about it—Watson ran right up his back. As they say in the business, 100 percent foul. But there was no call, even though the referee, John Pitti of Panama, was in direct line of the play, so he saw it clearly. His non-call was just poor officiating. So instead of a penalty kick in the early going and a great chance to make it 1–0 and force Costa Rica to open up play, we were left shaking our heads over a stinker of a call. That's soccer. As the play continued, we worked the ball well around the edge of the Costa Rica box until we created a kind of half chance for Christian in front. The cross came in at an angle where really it would have been very difficult for him to get around on it to put a shot on goal, and he skied it over the bar. But we had played well for the first twenty minutes, and should have had a penalty at least.

Then, disaster: at the twenty-nine-minute mark, Tim Howard

played the ball upfield, but it got cut off at midfield. The ball bounced straight to Bryan Ruiz, their best playmaker. Several of our players thought it was a hand ball and again looked for a call, and again didn't get one. Ruiz made a good pass to Marco Ureña, but still the play didn't look dangerous. Tim Ream and Geoff Cameron reacted slowly and gave Ureña some space, but not that much. Ream pushed him wide right, and it looked like a harmless position, but Ureña is a quality player: he slid a shot back across the goal toward the far post, and the ball somehow it made its way past Tim Howard. That's a play where we would expect our keeper could be in position to make a save, but it was a goal after a series of mistakes by our backline and our goalkeeper.

So now we were thirty minutes into a critical game. We didn't get a call on a key play at one end, and then, to their credit, Costa Rica created a goal out of almost nothing. I always say, "You need a little luck in these games." We weren't very lucky in the early going.

We'd wondered how much of a home-field advantage we'd have playing near New York, where teams from Central America tend to have strong followings. It was hard to know early in the game because everywhere you looked you saw Red Bull Arena packed with fans in red, white, and blue. Those are also the national colors of Costa Rica and once they scored, you saw those fans up and cheering and making their presence felt. Accounts differ on the breakdown at that game, but to me it felt like maybe fifty-fifty, as many Costa Rican fans as US fans there, or at least as vocal a contingent. I was having flashbacks to another US World Cup qualifying game I'd coached, back in 2001, sixteen years earlier to the day, when we hosted Honduras at RFK Stadium near Washington DC. I remember taking the field and looking up into the stands and seeing beautiful waves of blue in every direction I looked. We might as well have been playing in San

Pedro Sula, there were so many Hondurans there. We didn't feel we were the home team. We ended up losing that game against Honduras by one goal. I didn't blame the loss on the crowd then, and I don't now, but I still think it was a mistake to put our team in that kind of environment. Sixteen years later against Costa Rica, the problem wasn't as severe, but it was still a mistake to have that game at a stadium that neutralized our home-field advantage. US Soccer can't afford to continue to make easily fixable mistakes like that in the future.

"We need to create more chances," I told the guys at halftime. "We need to move the ball quicker. Make a play. Jump on a loose ball in the box. Make a cross. We just have to scrap and battle and put pressure on them."

We did that in the second half. Ream headed a corner kick over the crossbar, and despite a few aggressive attacks, we failed to deliver the final product. We'd known we'd have our hands full going against Costa Rica's outstanding keeper, Navas, and he made it hard on us. You're not the starting keeper for Real Madrid unless you're good, and he proved it that day. His reactions are quick, and he's also fast to come off his line and dominate the box. He showed it again at the sixty-seventh minute when Christian Pulisic launched a left-footed shot that deflected dangerously through the Costa Rica defense. In most games, against most keepers, that's a goal—but Navas made a pure reaction save that was spectacular, down on his butt, using both a hand and a foot.

Then in the eighty-first minute, Jozy came charging in past two defenders after a great delivery from Geoff Cameron, and they couldn't stop him, but Navas made another great save to block the shot. A minute later, Cameron gave a ball away in our defensive half, which sent Costa Rica's Marco Ureña through for his second goal of the game. Our hopes to grab a point were over, and the game ended 2–0.

It was a deflating loss. I believed this was a game from which we should have walked away with at least a point. However, poor concentration and play in a few moments of the game cost us dearly. We were simply not good enough. There is a fine line between winning and losing, and we were not up to the task. We didn't make any plays in the attacking end. We needed to be a little better on a couple of plays defensively. On the first goal, we made some mistakes, and we simply gifted them the second goal. I thought the officiating was poor, too. The Costa Ricans tried to slow the game down with a variety of antics, like feigning injuries and blatantly delaying play, and referee bought into all of it. They were the smarter team that day.

I talked to Christian after the game. He was hard on himself, and naturally he was disappointed, but that was all part of his growing experience. He'd been frustrated at times, and it had shown. Christian played with such love of the game, such joy and creativity, you wanted to make sure he held on to that. I didn't want to pack his head full of too many instructions. He was learning, growing as a player every game, and it was a pleasure to watch that development.

"You want to punish teams for fouls," I told Christian. "Get fouls that give us a penalty kick or dead-ball situations that are dangerous."

Typically, after these games, the press and social media swing into full-speed attacks on the coach and the team, and fair enough. I was a little startled that in the interview room afterward, with maybe a hundred reporters gathered, not one asked me about the Jozy Altidore penalty that wasn't given. You really wonder, *Do they watch the games?*

As a team and staff, we realized where the mistakes were made, and we pointed them out and moved forward. Planning for the game in Honduras was another tough challenge. Naturally, the team was down. But I told them we had a day to deal with the loss, and then we needed to move on to the game versus Honduras. I decided to keep training as light as possible through Sunday, and have a light training again on Monday in San Pedro Sula. The game-day conditions were going to be 91 degrees Fahrenheit with 80 percent humidity. The heat index was about 107 degrees.

I decided to start seven new players versus Honduras because I felt we needed the fittest players possible in the heat. The new additions would be Brad Guzan, Omar Gonzalez, Matt Besler, DaMarcus Beasley, Kellyn Acosta, Clint Dempsey, and Jordan Morris. Graham Zusi, Michael Bradley, Darlington Nagbe, and Christian Pulisic would be holdovers in the first eleven. I believed in our roster. We would have fit and experienced players on the field and a number of good options to bring off the bench in the second half. I used our charter flight from Newark to San Pedro Sula to meet with all the players individually to explain the plan.

Things went badly. Despite having an edge in play, we fell behind in the first half when at the twenty-seven-minute mark Honduran and Houston Dynamo player Romell Quioto beat both Graham Zusi and Omar Gonzalez and put a well-placed shot past Brad Guzan. At that point, the team became discouraged and closed out the half in poor form. This was not good. The conditions were difficult, and we needed everyone to get their heads in the right place if we had a chance of leaving this stadium with at least a point. I used the halftime break to rally the troops with a few choice words, and alerted the team to potential changes in players and formation in the second half.

The second half was extremely challenging. The effects of the heat and humidity drained both teams. The game was not pretty, and closing it out was going to require a lot of mental and physical toughness. We simply needed to battle and find a play to equalize. I made two changes around the sixty-two-minute mark, bringing

Geoff Cameron and Paul Arriola into the game and switching to a 3-4-2-1 formation. We were beginning to have more possession and create some chances.

Bobby Wood entered the game at the seventy-three-minute mark. By then both teams were simply trying to endure; as if the heat wasn't bad enough, the referee decided to abandon the second-half water break, as well. We stayed in it, and at the eighty-sixth minute, a brilliant direct free kick by Acosta led to an even better save by the Honduran keeper Luis López. As the ball bounced around, Jordan Morris moved superbly to keep it alive, and after a flick-on by Matt Besler, Bobby Wood showed his skill by controlling the ball with his chest and then burying it in the back of the net. The referee decided there would only be three minutes of added time after a game that warranted many more, due to substitutions, injuries, cards, etc. However, we gladly took the point, keeping our World Cup dreams alive.

This result gave us a great point. We showed character in a game in which there were many things we could blame for getting a bad result—the heat and humidity, the 3:30 p.m. kickoff, the field, the officiating, and on and on. Our guys hung in there. I knew qualification would go down to the last game, and that was where we stood looking ahead to our last two games in the Hex, at home versus Panama on October 6 and away at Trinidad four days later.

COUNTRY	POINTS	GOAL DIFFERENTIAL
Mexico	18	+8, qualified
Costa Rica	15	+7
Panama	10	+2
USA	9	+1
Honduras	9	-7
Trinidad	3	-11

The Hex had been a long and winding road with some ups and downs for the US team. This is what CONCACAF World Cup qualifying is all about. Just ask Mexico in 2013, when they qualified for the 2014 World Cup on the last day, being rewarded by a Graham Zusi goal in the ninety-third minute against Panama, which sent Mexico to the World Cup. Over the past six months, we had fought to be in a position to qualify. We needed to win the next two games, against Panama and Trinidad; if we did, we qualified. It was up to us. We couldn't ask for more.

My Worst Day

We arrived in Orlando, Florida, on the Sunday before the Friday night game against Panama and had four days in camp together to prepare for it. It was a light week of training. Coming off the disappointing home loss to Costa Rica and the tie in Honduras, I was determined to be even more thorough in our preparations for these last two games. Our evaluation of our player pool and past results told me a couple of things. One was that I had made a mistake going into the Costa Rica game in selecting a large number of our European-based players to start— Geoff Cameron, Tim Ream, Fabian Johnson, Bobby Wood, and Christian Pulisic.

There was no doubt about the quality of these players. However, I was not as focused as I should have been on the fact that they were just starting their club seasons, which meant they were a long way from gaining full fitness and sharpness. In addition, we had a full complement of players from our winning Gold Cup squad who had a better feel for each other and were sharp and fit because they were fully immersed in their MLS campaigns. My thinking at the time had been that if I were to use the European-based players in that set of games, the first game versus Costa Rica would be a better fit for them, because of the better playing surface on a US field and less heat and humidity. The second game versus Honduras would be very challenging with the travel, poor field, and heat and humidity. Therefore, I took a calculated risk—but I failed. The team I chose to start in Honduras included only one European-based player, Christian, in our first eleven, and I think we fielded a team that was better suited on the day to get us a badly needed point, which kept us alive in qualifying.

Planning for Panama, I wanted fit players, and players with pace. In making final selections, I wanted players who had been getting regular minutes with their club teams over the past three weeks. I also looked for those who could help us build a good team spirit over the ten days we would be together in camp. The best twenty-six players are rarely the best formula for success; there needs to be a balance. At this level, it's natural for everyone to want to play. These are players of quality and they are very competitive people. However, they need to understand their roles and have a strong desire for the *team* to succeed, and they need to separate themselves mentally from their club teams. The truth is that a national team is different from a club team. We do things differently and employ different tactics. Player roles are different. If we're to be successful, it's essential that the group buys into all of this.

The game plan for Panama was simple: we would be aggressive. Panama had established a very impressive defensive record in the Hex, conceding only five goals in eight games. We needed to be on our front foot to break them down, so we went with an attacking 4-1-3-2 formation to start the game. We would push five players in advanced positions—Jozy Altidore, Bobby Wood, Christian Pulisic, Darlington Nagbe, and Paul Arriola. Michael Bradley would be charged with organizing our midfield shape.

Our backline and goalkeeper would consist of Jorge Villafaña, Matt Besler, Omar Gonzalez, DeAndre Yedlin, and Tim Howard. Eight of our starters had played key roles in winning the Gold Cup.

My old friend Bob Bradley and I had been seeing more of each other in recent months. He was back in Manhattan Beach in his new job building a Major League Soccer expansion team in Los Angeles, LAFC. We go way back, not just coaching together, but spending family vacations together for years. Over dinner I'd mentioned the idea of inviting him to the next national team camp.

Bob arrived in camp the Wednesday before the game against Panama, and I knew his presence would be a plus for us. I also wanted to start to build a tradition in US national soccer whereby former national team coaches aren't shunned, but are welcomed back out of respect for their contributions to the game and the program. That could apply to any former US national team coach, if the timing was right. (Bob was great to have around. He left the morning after the Panama game. He watched the game upstairs for us and made some comments at halftime. It was good to get another voice on some things.)

Every game is different. Sometimes it all clicks from the beginning, and that was how the Panama game went. The plan to have Christian, Jozy, and Bobby press the action together created havoc. They couldn't have been more in sync. On the first goal, just eight minutes into the game, Bobby flicked the ball to Jozy, who laid it off to Christian, who took the ball in stride with the inside of his left foot, played it past the Panamanian central defense, then pushed it past goalkeeper Jaime Penedo and scored from a sharp angle. We had the home crowd rollicking after that. Then in the nineteenth minute, Darlington Nagbe played a ball behind Panama's right back that Christian received in stride, then beat defender Michael Murillo one-on-one in the final third and slid a left-footed cross right in front of the goal for Jozy to slot for our second goal in the first twenty minutes. For the third goal, Bobby Wood beat a couple of Panamanian defenders and was fouled in the box to set up a penalty kick by Jozy Altidore. We cruised in the second half, Bobby Wood adding one more goal off a Paul Arriola assist, and completed a dominant performance, winning by an impressive 4–0 score. Costa Rica and Honduras played to a draw the same night, so we were back in third place in the Hex and positioned to earn an automatic spot in the World Cup with a third-place finish if we could go to Trinidad and win or tie to pick up at least one point.

The end was in sight. It had seemed at times as if we'd never see the last day of qualifying. As a team, we'd been through so many pressure moments. I remembered how critical the game versus Honduras back in March had been to our program. If we'd failed to win on that day, there was a pretty good chance our hopes for Russia would have been shot right then. I took nothing for granted—you seldom do as a coach—but after the strong game against Panama, it felt like *Russia, here we come!*

I was confident we'd get the result we needed, but I never expected an easy game. There are no easy games in CONCACAF qualifying, especially not on the road. My experience told me that Trinidad and Tobago would give us a good game. They'd been a little unlucky in the Hex, failing to get results in games where they deserved better. In their last match in Mexico, they led the best team in CONCACAF for seventy-eight minutes, then fell 3–1. I warned our team after the game versus Panama that we needed to be ready to play.

We traveled to Trinidad after a light training session in Orlando on Sunday, October 8. We were scheduled to have a training session on the stadium field on Monday morning, the day before the game. Upon our arrival at the venue, we discovered the field had been flooded by an overnight storm. The CONCACAF match commissioner had not bothered to inform us of this issue. The whole track was in puddles and guys didn't want to ruin their boots by soaking them, so players had to be carried out there just to train. We had a light jog and played some small possession games and went back to our hotel. I didn't think the lack of practice would be an issue but figured the light day would probably benefit us because guys were still tired from the game against Panama and traveling down to Port of Spain.

As I've said, to Trinidad's credit, in their previous qualifying game, they'd led Mexico for seventy-five minutes—in Mexico. We knew we were facing a team with the potential to beat us. We went into the game hoping that because they had no way to qualify for the World Cup they would come into the game light on motivation. Instead, the opposite happened. For whatever reason, pictures of our training session on the flooded practice field went out on our social media platforms. There were shots of players being carried out onto the field and of us practicing behind the goal. The Trinidad federation felt embarrassed and humiliated. It's fine to use social media to help fans keep up with the team and get excited about games, but there's a way to do that without making anyone look bad. The bottom line is, by embarrassing them we helped fire up Trinidad for a game that meant nothing to them. Bad idea.

The coaching staff prepared edits on the Panama game, as well as presenting our scouting reports and videos on Trinidad. The medical staff, fitness coach, and trainers reported on the fitness status of all players. We had two injury concerns: Jozy Altidore and Christian Pulisic. But the day before the game, Jozy was cleared to play, and on game day, Christian passed his fitness test. We would have a full complement of players available for the game.

As a staff, we considered a couple of changes to our first eleven from the game versus Panama. Perhaps Brad Guzan for Tim Howard in the goal? Tim looked good in training and we decided to play him. He was coming off a shutout, his forty-second for the US national team, second on the all-time list only to Kasey Keller's forty-seven. Perhaps a change in our backline? Insert Cameron, Ream, or Beasley? A change in the midfield? Bedoya or Acosta? Dempsey for Wood or Altidore? In the end, we decided on no changes. The first eleven all recovered well from the game against Panama, which was arguably our best performance since our game against Costa Rica in the semifinals of the Gold Cup, and eight of these players had started in that game. The exceptions would be Pulisic, Wood, and Yedlin.

Game plans are a funny thing. At times, you're right on target, and other times you scrap them minutes into the game. The plan against Trinidad was to be aggressive from the kickoff. We would play the same eleven as we did versus Panama with a slight adjustment. Nagbe and Arriola would start the game playing closer to Michael Bradley. Therefore, our 4-1-3-2 formation would slant more towards a 4-4-2 diamond. The thinking was to simply keep it a little tighter in the midfield by offering more support to Michael. In the attack, Villafaña and Yedlin could offer width.

As I did in our preparation for the Panama game, I preached a dos-and-don'ts list to the team. The dos and don'ts are generally ten or so things that we need to reinforce about what we needed to do in the game. The don'ts were reminders of things we couldn't do, and this was hammered again and again over the three days of preparation.

Here's the DON'T list we emphasized for the game:

- UNDERESTIMATE OUR OPPONENT.
- Get sent off. Be smart and disciplined.
- Play backward when you can play forward.
- Concede fouls and free kicks in our defensive third.
- Be undisciplined on the defensive side of the ball.
- Be surprised by anything.

And the DO list:

- Play smart, be aggressive.
- Press high early in the game.
- Be aggressive in the attacking third and be prepared for the counterattack.

Coaching is an interesting business. You have elite players whom you mold into a team over a period of time, during short windows at various times in the year. If you do things right and learn from your mistakes, you start to build a cohesive team. They begin to understand their strengths and weaknesses. They develop leadership, support each other, and become committed to the cause. Going into the Trinidad game, I really thought we were making progress, and I thought with another six to eight months to prepare, we would have a better team to play in the 2018 World Cup. I expected good things to happen on the field that day. It just didn't work out that way.

We started the game sluggishly and still created a very good chance in the seventh minute, but Jozy hit it over the crossbar. The field was playing slow, but we'd known going into the game that the field wouldn't play particularly well. Our passing was poor and our effort looked worse. In my view, we screwed up too many plays and were losing too many individual battles in the first fifteen minutes of the game. Then in the seventeenth minute came the moment no one will ever forget.

A cross from the right flank caught defender Omar Gonzalez off-balance and his attempt to clear the ball went wrong, twisting miserably off his foot and hooking up and down and right into the goal, catching a surprised Tim Howard off guard. It was the kind of freak mistake you could spend ten years trying to duplicate but never doing so. In all my years of coaching, I'd never seen an own goal like that, and I'm sure I'll never see one to top it.

That goal gave Trinidad the lead and a sense of belief that they could beat us that day. I felt that if we got in at halftime down a goal, we could reorganize the team and get the result we needed in the second half. We started to slightly grow into the game over the next twenty minutes until Trinidad's right back Alvin Jones moved the ball up the right side. I remember the play very clearly because it happened right in front of me. Jones shaped up to shoot from more than thirty-five yards away, and I said to myself, "This guy can't be shooting at goal." But shoot he did. It was incredibly well struck and had pace and movement. It knuckled a little on Tim Howard and hit the side panel of the goal to his right. On a better day, I would like to believe that Tim could get a hand on that shot. Not that day.

That sent us into the locker room down 2–0 at halftime. I'd rarely had to verbally get after the team during my eleven months in charge, but this time there was a lot of yelling, not only by me. We demanded better of each other for the second half. I told them we needed to fight and start winning our battles, that we needed to get the next goal in the game and if we did we would get the result we needed.

I brought Clint Dempsey into the game for Paul Arriola to start the second half, and pushed Christian Pulisic to the right side to give him more space to attack Trinidad's backline. At the forty-seven-minute mark, Christian scored from twenty yards out off an assist from Darlington Nagbe. We were back in the game. At that point, I felt confident we could get the second goal. We kept up the pressure, but Trinidad was not going to make it easy for us.

We changed to a 3-4-3 when Kellyn Acosta entered the game at the seventy-two-minute mark. Trinidad was smart about killing time with a number of stoppages for alleged injuries. We created a few good chances, which were thwarted by their goalkeeper, Adrian Foncette. Benny Feilhaber, who entered the game in the eighty-forth minute, had a header from five yards out that was probably our best scoring chance, but Foncette made the save.

Our last best effort was Clint Dempsey, who hit the post in the closing minutes. It wasn't to be. The game ended 2–1 in favor of Trinidad and Tobago. We'd been working together for eleven months, and our dreams of playing the World Cup were over, just like that.

There is not much you can say to a team after a game like that. I thanked the players and made it clear that the failure was on all of us and there would be no finger pointing. I couldn't help thinking that our nineteen-year old sensation, Christian Pulisic, would not be seeing his first World Cup in 2018. It wasn't fair. He'd had a tremendous qualifying campaign, and the world needed to see this young talent. I thought about our fans, who have been steadfast supporters of the national team. I thought about our sponsors, who were positioned to rally behind us. I thought about our coaching staff, who gave up other jobs to support me, placing their careers and livelihood in jeopardy in this challenge of trying to qualify our team for Russia.

I also had a moment of peace, knowing we had given everything we had for this struggle. We knew we'd take a beating in the press. This was a stunning setback. At times like that, it means even more when people reach out. In particular, I remember a note sent to me by Don Garber, the MLS Commissioner, reading, "Success is not final, failure is not fatal: it is the courage to continue that counts." I knew we would continue, and come back stronger.

I went back to the bar at the Hyatt Regency with Matt Reis, our goalkeeper coach, and Martha Romero, my assistant, and stayed there talking until late, drinking a bottle of wine. Jay Berhalter, number three in US Soccer, stopped by and was asking about the upcoming games in November. I tried to tell Jay I wasn't going to be with the team anymore in November. After he left, a whole group of US fans stopped by and thanked me for what I'd done for US soccer. They told me they were going to keep supporting the team.

I had two or three hours sleep that night and caught the team charter from Port of Spain to Miami. I remember, as we were coming off the flight, I was walking next to Christian, giving him a little room because he was so beat up. He was a real man in qualifying. He got kicked so much and was so banged up, he had a hard time sitting down on the plane.

"You mind if I stay in touch and drop you a line now and then?" I asked Christian.

"No problem," he said.

We walked in silence for a few paces.

"This is now your team," I told Christian. "You can't allow what happened yesterday to happen again."

He just nodded, and that was enough.

Part V

A Bold Plan for the Future

The American Problem

After the US team's stunning loss to Trinidad and Tobago in 2017, dreams of playing in the 2018 World Cup were suddenly a thing of the past. Soccer is now widely accepted and clearly has a great future in our country. On the commercial side, it is growing impressively—in television ratings, sponsorships, attendance, cultural relevance, you name it. Yet on the field there are still enough issues that I have serious concerns. We need to talk these issues through and come to some consensus, or we'll be forever stuck repeating the same mistakes.

One thing is clear: the problems and issues we have now in 2018 are the same ones we had the day before we played Trinidad and Tobago, and they were the same the day after. If you don't agree with that, then you are either in denial or you don't understand the issues.

For a start, we have a huge void in the leadership of the sport in this country, specifically a lack of expertise in the technical side of the game, and that lack undermines any progress we are trying to make on the field of play. We need to improve our coaching, our coaching education, and the administrative leadership of the sport. We also need to avoid listening to the opinions of every Tom, Dick, and Harry. If we begin to make things better by getting the right people in the right places, the sport will grow and get better, and some of the loudmouths might not be heard as much as they are today.

Back in the 1980s, I was taking my refresher course in the A-level coaching school held by US Soccer in Tampa, Florida. Former national team coach Walt Chyzowych, the director of coaching for the federation, gave the course's opening talk, titled "The American Problem." Walt said: "We are geographically a very big country: we have three different time zones, we have different climates, we have different cultures and languages. Yes, we can take bits and pieces from everyone, but ultimately, we need to find our own way of mastering this game. We are simply different from the rest of the world, and therefore trying to copy Holland, England, Spain, France, Italy, Germany, Brazil, or Argentina makes no sense. We have to find our own solutions to our own set of problems. We are unique, we are different from the rest of the world, and we should not be copying anyone else."

Three decades later, I'm not sure we've ever really heeded Walt's wise words, and as a result, sadly, we simply have not made the kind of progress we should have made in the technical side of the game. We're still looking for solutions to the American problem.

Where do we start? What do we need to do to get better?

Let's look at the professional game in our country. In 1996, we started Major League Soccer, based on an agreement with FIFA for having been awarded the 1994 World Cup in the United States. FIFA felt that the United States was the last frontier they needed to conquer to really make soccer the "world's game." They wanted the biggest and richest country in the world to be truly a part of the FIFA family, and starting the MLS was seen as a very important step toward that goal.

I can tell you that when we kicked off the league, we were nowhere near prepared to handle all the challenges of such a major endeavor. The league and its local markets scrambled to get strong ownership in place. We began with ten teams: the New England Revolution, the New York/New Jersey MetroStars, Washington DC United, the Tampa Bay Mutiny, the Kansas City Wiz, the Columbus Crew, the Colorado Rapids, the Dallas Burn, the San Jose Clash, and the LA Galaxy. With a strong influence of NFL owners—the Kraft Family (New England) and Lamar Hunt (Kansas City and Columbus), plus John Kluge and Stuart Subotnick (MetroStars) and Phil Anschutz (Colorado)—among a variety of other ownership groups, as well as league-operated franchises in Tampa, Dallas, and San Jose, the league kicked off in 1996 under its single-entity business model. Typical of any professional league in its inaugural season, there were countless issues, from poor stadiums and poor day-to-day management to poor travel, poor officiating, and poor leadership. However, we had some surprisingly good players in the league. It was a start.

At the time, when I accepted the head coach and assistant general manager positions at DC United, I was excited that we were kicking off a new professional league in the United States. I was excited that we would be giving our American players the chance to play and become solid professionals, and I was excited that we would be growing soccer to the point where one day we would challenge the rest of the world by positioning ourselves to win a World Cup.

Because of its aggressive deputy commissioner, Sunil Gulati, the league was able to sign some international players with huge reputations and some good playing years still ahead of them, like Carlos Valderrama, Marco Etcheverry, Roberto Donadoni, and Jorge Campos. Some top American players came home to play in MLS, too, including John Harkes, Tab Ramos, Eric Wynalda, and Alexi Lalas. There was good momentum and for the most part we put up a pretty good smoke screen to cover up our many shortcomings, but there would be a lot of work that needed to get done for the league to flourish.

"The guys who started the league . . . don't know soccer," Eric Wynalda commented at the time. "They screwed up in the most vital part possible, which is in how the game is presented."

Leadership comes in all different shapes, sizes, and forms. I think all organizations require good leadership, whether you're talking about business, politics, sports, education, or religion, but just what constitutes good leadership seems to remain a mystery to many people. When things are going well, great, everyone's happy, and sometimes leaders are given more credit than they deserve. When things are not going well, you better have good leaders in your organization, and they need to be the kind of people who are willing to accept the responsibility when things are not going well.

In my opinion, NFL Commissioner Roger Goodell is an example of someone who is not a good leader. His poor handling of a number of issues in recent years, from sexual abuse cases to "deflate-gate," has clearly damaged the reputation of the league. Yet the NFL is arguably the most successful professional sports league in the world. I thought George W. Bush (9/11) and Barack Obama (the aftermath of the 2007–2008 financial crisis) were outstanding leaders in difficult times. Our soccer leadership needs to be better, that is, more than spokespeople or persons positioned on a corporate ladder. Good leaders have vision and perspective. They identify problems and solve them. They follow up and make sure those solutions have been implemented. They also take care to hire the right people and design organizations accordingly. In the end, you will have an organization running on all cylinders, positioned to deal with any problems that may come your way. You should never be blindsided.

Soccer in the United States is growing at all levels, but it will take many more years before we can relax a bit and feel good about where we are. We'll reach that point only with strong, smart, and decisive leadership focused on continuing to chase our goals of successfully competing at the international levels and battling for acceptance in our own country.

So who are the leaders in our sport? How do they lead? What are their strengths? What are their weaknesses? Can we be successful with these types of leaders?

Here's the blunt truth: our two largest entities in the sport, US Soccer and MLS, are run by people with limited technical knowledge of the sport. They have commercial, financial, and political strengths but lack a strong understanding of the game on the field, and even worse, they have not surrounded themselves with people who can make up for their deficiencies.

Unlike many of the other professional leagues in our country, the MLS does not have the advantage of a feeder system coming out of the intercollegiate ranks. For the most part, the MLS and US Soccer are taking on a large responsibility in player development, and these responsibilities affect the national team program. Therefore I strongly believe we need more experienced people in leadership to help complement the work that is being done at MLS clubs and at amateur clubs throughout the country. I do believe we have more talented players than ever before. However, there is a huge hole in our development scheme for players between the ages of seventeen and twenty-one. We need better opportunities and competition for these players so we can properly develop them for senior competition. I believe this will require that we have more experienced people in the game to help improve these programs. In time, we will improve the development of the American player and thus benefit our national team programs.

The bylaws of the United States Soccer Federation, Inc. state the following:

Bylaw 102. Purposes

The purposes of the Federation are:

1. to promote, govern, coordinate and administer the growth and development of soccer in all its recognized forms in the United States for all persons of all ages and abilities, including national teams and international games and tournaments;
2. to provide for the continuing development of soccer players, coaches, referees and administrators;
3. to provide for national cup competitions; and
4. to provide for the prompt and equitable resolution of grievances.

My concerns center on purpose number 2: the development of soccer players, coaches, referees, and administrators. This is clearly the technical side or sporting side of the federation. US Soccer has been led by President Sunil Gulati, CEO/Secretary General Dan Flynn, and Chief Commercial Director Jay Berhalter. They are the key individuals in the organization, and for the most part they are responsible for all commercial, financial, and technical decisions. I think very highly of these three guys. They have worked tirelessly for the sport and love the game. However, I don't believe they have the technical expertise to make the technical decisions that they need to make. Keep in mind that the president is not a paid employee of US Soccer. He is not responsible for the day-to-day running of the organization. I believe his role is one of helping set policy, representing the federation, and having a strong public presence. Sunil, Dan, and Jay strongly influence all the technical decisions at US Soccer, and I believe this has led to some poor decisions in policies and programs at the federation level. These poor decisions have hurt the sport.

After our disappointing loss versus Trinidad and Tobago in World Cup qualifier, I spent a good two hours talking about the organization of US Soccer with Carlos Cordeiro, the vice president of the organization. Carlos has had a very successful career in business on Wall Street and elsewhere and has in the later stages of his life acquired a deeper interest in the sport of soccer. I told Carlos on the flight back from Trinidad that there was a real void in the guidance and support of the national team program. There were no clear lines of responsibility as to how the pieces were to fit together and, for the most part, I was left on my own.

My predecessor, Jürgen Klinsmann, had much more authority and power on paper, with the title of technical director. However, the reality was that US Soccer in Chicago made most of the technical decisions. I told Carlos that I strongly believed that the federation needed to have a general manager for the senior national team and also a technical director in the organization.

The general manager would oversee all facets of the program, offering great assistance to the head coach and the federation. Responsibilities would include setting up guidelines and procedures on how the program operates, helping select coaches, mentoring the coaches, coordinating all departments of US Soccer that directly affect the soccer program itself, and even more important, having a voice in commercial decisions that affect the senior team. A general manager would help create clear lines of communication among the top officials of US Soccer and the national team program. I believe the position would help create a more efficient organization and allow for optimal results.

The technical director would manage coaching education, sports science, and the academy programs. In US Soccer House, the headquarters buildings in Chicago, very few people have responsibility over all the many technical aspects of the business. Having only a few people with experience and responsibility does not allow the business to run in an optimal manner. Things need to change.

One clear example of poor communication and mismanagement were some of the decisions in selecting venues for our home games in World Cup qualifying. For me, these were critical decisions. How were these decisions made? Who had input in the decision-making process? Who was ultimately responsible for these decisions?

In 2017, I was able to speak up at the last minute and help change the venue from Salt Lake City to San Jose for our home game versus Honduras. Playing a critically important game at high altitude with an 0-2 record would have been a disaster. We won the game 6–0 and got ourselves back in contention to qualify for the 2018 World Cup. I questioned the venue for the Costa Rica game, too, because many Costa Rica fans live in the New York area and were sure to show up in large, enthusiastic numbers, but I was told we were too far down the road, and others were certain the venue would be a positive for our team. I had my doubts, and the venue we chose to play Costa Rica (Red Bull Stadium in Newark, New Jersey) was a poor choice. We played one of the best teams in CONCACAF in arguably one of the most comfortable geographical locations for them in the United States. We lost the game 2–0, and it would be very unfair to attribute the loss to the venue. We needed to play better on the day, but most observers reckoned that the crowd was at least fifty-fifty, rather than giving us raucous home support. These types of decisions are critical and can make the difference in qualifying for a World Cup.

After the 2014–2018 campaign, we should realize that there is a very fine line between qualifying for the World Cup and narrowly missing out. In the future, we need to get all these decisions right, including seemingly small details, and to do that we have to have the right type of management team in place. We no longer have any margin for error. Unlike other countries, the United States does not have a home stadium for the national team. We also have an incredibly diverse population, which comprises many immigrants from the homelands of our competitors. We need to make the right decisions in venue selections, and all voices need to be heard. Having a general manager in place will ensure that these decisions are made in collaboration with the management of the national team program and that these types of missteps never happen again.

I do want to be clear: I think US Soccer and MLS have done a very good job in moving the sport forward. They have promoted and built it. US Soccer provides for player, coach, and referee development. MLS has impressively grown the professional league. However, that progress goes only so far. We need to get better if we wish to one day compete to win a World Cup. I don't believe either organization has done a good job in developing senior-level administrators. Basically, the same people have remained in control of the sport over the past twenty years. This should not happen. The landscape of the sport has changed drastically, and there is a need for new leaders with technical experience who can bring fresh ideas to the table. There needs to be some new blood and some new ways of doing things.

I don't think we need wholesale changes. However, we need good experienced people to play important roles in our leading entities in the sport.

Let me offer an example in another sport. After retiring as the manager of the Los Angeles Dodgers, Joe Torre was appointed executive vice president for baseball operations by Major League Baseball. Joe Torre's experience and knowledge are unquestionable. He has the respect of everyone in the sport and has a positive influence on the day-to-day functioning of MLB. Having this type of person involved in the technical side of the game is a real plus. Do we have people of this quality in senior management positions in either US Soccer or MLS? The sport of soccer is very deficient in this critically important area.

To further make my point, turning to MLS, I see many of the same issues as I do with US Soccer. The commissioner, Don Garber, has a background in sports marketing with the NFL. The deputy commissioner, Mark Abbott, is a trained lawyer and a very competent professional. Senior vice president Todd Durbin is a trained lawyer with an expertise in contracts. These gentlemen are the top decision makers in the league but have very little technical expertise, and the ones who have a technical background have only small voices in league policy.

The MLS follows the NFL model in the way it implements policy and makes the decisions that affect the product on the field. There are a number of league committees who are charged with making suggestions on the technical side; however, few of these get implemented in the right ways. Clearly the owners have the loudest voices and typically make decisions without the best information. I believe this hurts the league. Keep in mind that there are big differences between the sports of football and soccer. On the technical side, the NFL answers to no one, while the MLS has to answer to a number of governing bodies (FIFA, CONCACAF, US Soccer, etc.). The NFL can implement any rule its officials feel is in its best interests and answer to basically no one. It could make a touchdown worth ten points and a field goal worth five. The NFL has no competition in the sport, while MLS competes globally. The sport of soccer is a complicated business, and it continues to get more challenging every year. The technical management of the sport in our country requires changes; more experienced people need to be placed in positions of responsibility in these areas. Knowledge and experience in the game are critical for our future leadership. For our sport to move forward, our leadership needs to have an expertise in business, politics, *and* the technical and sporting aspects of the game. One without the others does not work.

The Shrinking Pool

As we look into the future of the US Soccer National Team Program, we need to examine our domestic players in MLS and the roles they play and contributions they provide to their club teams. Speaking as the former national team coach, I hope that these players will make up a strong nucleus of our roster and pool of players. In addition, those who are playing outside of MLS, whether in Europe or Mexico or elsewhere, should be important additions to the overall pool as well.

My concern is that the quality in the pool of players in MLS is diminishing. One would think that, as the league continues to expand, there would be more opportunities for the American player and that the national team pool of domestic players would be expanding. However, as you look at the twelve teams that qualified for the MLS playoffs in 2017, it appears that only about 34 percent of the starters for these teams were even eligible to play for the US national team, and out of this group, only a small percentage were of the caliber to be considered in the national team pool. That's scary stuff!

Below, I've listed the starting players from these teams who would be eligible to play for the US national team. Keep in mind that I've chosen only the first games these teams played in the 2017 playoffs, and there could be other eligible players who were not chosen due to injuries or suspensions, or because they were not in their team's starting lineup.

CHICAGO (4)	NEW YORK RED BULLS (5)	VANCOUVER WHITECAPS (1)
Matt Lampson (GK)	Luis Robles (GK)	Tim Parker
Matt Polster	Sacha Kljestan	
Brandon Vincent	Sean Davis	
Dax McCarty	Tyler Adams	
	Aaron Long	

SAN JOSE (5)	ATLANTA (2)	COLUMBUS (4)
Andrew Tarbell (GK)	Brad Guzan (GK)	Zack Steffen (GK)
Kofi Sarkodie	Jeff Larentowicz	Josh Williams
Shea Salinas		Héctor Jiménez
Chris Wondolowski		Wil Trapp
Tommy Thompson		

HOUSTON (3)	SPORTING KC (5)	SEATTLE (5)
Tyler Deric (GK)	Andrew Dykstra (GK)	Stefan Frei (GK)
DaMarcus Beasley	Graham Zusi	Chad Marshall
Ricardo Clark	Ike Opara	Cristian Roldan
	Matt Besler	Harry Shipp
	Benny Feilhaber	Will Bruin

TORONTO (6)	NYCFC (3)	PORTLAND (2)
Jozy Altidore	Sean Johnson (GK)	Jeff Attinella (GK)
Eriq Zavaleta	Ethan White	Darlington Nagbe
Drew Moor	Ben Sweat	
Marco Delgado		
Michael Bradley		
Justin Morrow		

In summary, out of the twelve MLS playoff teams, starting players who were eligible to play for the US national team totaled forty-five, of whom ten were goalkeepers. On average, there were 3.75 eligible players starting per MLS playoff team. Looking at this a little more closely, 29 percent of the field players were eligible and 83 percent of the goalkeepers. In all, only about one out of three starters was eligible to play for the US.

As I examine this pool of forty-five players, a total of fourteen would be in my plans. A number of these players are at the end of their international careers, and there are very few young players. We need to know the reasons for this troubling situation.

To look more closely, let's think about two of the teams that failed to make the playoffs in 2017. In the last game of the regular season, on October 22, the team with the worst record in the league, the LA Galaxy, lost at FC Dallas, 5–1, to conclude the season for both teams. The starting lineups for these teams totaled only seven players who would be eligible to play for the US national team. These players were:

DALLAS	LA
Jesse Gonzalez (GK)	Bradford "BJ" Jamieson
Matt Hedges	Jermaine Jones
Ryan Hollingshead	Dave Romney
Kellyn Acosta	

This is a troubling trend that needs to be addressed. In 2017, players from sixty-seven different countries played in MLS. US-born players are being squeezed out of the picture. The percentage of US-born players has dropped from 62.3 percent in 1996, when the league started, to 52.1 percent in 2014, and then to 43.5 percent in 2017. Some clubs carry as many as fifteen international players on their rosters. In the MLS opening game of 2017, Portland against Minnesota, the combined starting lineups had only three players who were eligible to play for the US national team.

I was at the game, standing next to Don Garber, and made the point to him at the time. Don just shrugged.

In a February 26, 2018, article projecting the Major League Soccer opening-day lineups for the 2018 season, *Soccer America* editor in chief Paul Kennedy wrote, "Only three of twenty-three teams are projected to start a majority of players eligible for the US national team. Toronto FC and Seattle, which met in the MLS Cup 2017, lead all teams, with seven Americans. The fewest: New York City FC, with one American in the starting lineup (goalkeeper Sean Johnson) and Portland, with none." It was projected that, from the twenty-three teams, a total of eighty-seven Americans would be starters, about 29 percent of the total available starting positions; and in my view perhaps twenty-five of these players would be considered in the national team pool of players. A pretty sad statement.

In recent years, Major League Soccer has increased funding to help teams strengthen their rosters. This program, TAM (targeted allocation money), has considerably increased the recruitment of international players. At the same time, the salary cap budget for teams has grown at a rate of 5 percent annually, which typically fails to cover annual inflation of salaries. Therefore, someone is getting squeezed out, and it has been the American player. Americans are playing less and typically are paid considerably less than their international counterparts. There are exceptions: players like Michael Bradley, Jozy Altidore, Clint Dempsey, and Tim Howard make good money. All in all, however, the league has strongly moved toward a more pronounced international player influence.

Keep in mind that the mission of MLS is to grow the league both commercially and technically. Doing this will improve future television deals, sponsorships, and profitabilty. League officials are not focused on developing the American player, despite the fact that the academy programs continue to grow. There need to be some changes. The governing body of the sport in the United States, US Soccer, needs to step in and try to counteract this trend. After all, the goal of US Soccer should be to govern the sport, grow the sport, support the sport, and grow the national team programs. The current trend in MLS is not favorable to the goals of US Soccer.

Past, Present, and Future

In October 2017, Claudio Reyna and I had some beers together on a beautiful afternoon in Charlottesville, Virginia, right across from the Rotunda at the University of Virginia. We were in town to celebrate the twenty-fifth anniversary of our 1992 NCAA Division One National Championship. For me, it's always a rewarding experience to see my former players and marvel at their successes in life. Seeing Claudio helped take away from some of the hurt and disappointment I was experiencing over the loss in Trinidad.

Claudio captained the US team in the 2002 and 2006 World Cups. After a beer or two, he and I enjoyed comparing the 2002 team to the 2017 team. Let's be fair: we were comparing the best team in our soccer history to one of the most disappointing ones. You'd never know that from watching TV, of course, where you're liable to hear just about anything, even the claim that in 2017 our pool was the most talented in the history of US soccer.

Today's game is different, faster and with better conditioned athletes, but we still play with the same ball, and the field is still the same shape. Are the players representing the United States today any better than those who did so in the past?

STARTING TEAM VERSUS GERMANY IN THE QUARTER-FINALS OF THE 2002 WORLD CUP

G
Brad Friedel

D Tony Sanneh   **D** Eddie Pope   **D** Gregg Berhalter   **D** Frankie Hejduk

M Pablo Mastroeni   **M** John O'Brien

M Claudio Reyna   **M** Eddie Lewis

F Brian McBride   **F** Landon Donovan

RESERVES USED: Clint Mathis, Cobi Jones, Earnie Stewart

Claudio and I were unanimous in our opinion: we would both take the 2002 team over the 2017 team as a whole—and take almost every player from that team over his 2017 counterpart. In fact, we both felt that only one player from 2017 had an edge over his 2002 counterpart, Christian Pulisic. I also think that Michael Bradley would compete for a place in the first eleven.

Keep in mind, I coached both teams. I believe the 2017 team lacked consistent quality at both ends of the field. In the attack, with the exception of Christian Pulisic, we rarely had a player with the speed on and off the ball to get by opponents. Defensively, we never found the best center-back combinations, and what is traditionally a US strength, goalkeeping, was not there in our two losses in 2017. As coaches, we always talk about players who can "make plays" in big games, and we simply did not have

STARTING TEAM VERSUS TRINIDAD AND TOBAGO IN

THE FINAL GAME OF THE HEX IN OCTOBER 2017

G
Tim Howard

D	**D**	**D**	**D**
DeAndre Yedlin	Omar Gonzalez	Matt Besler	Jorge Villafaña

M
Michael Bradley

M	**M**	**M**
Paul Arriola	Christian Pulisic	Darlington Nagbe

F	**F**
Bobby Wood	Jozy Altidore

RESERVES USED: Clint Dempsey, Kellyn Acosta, Benny Feilhaber

enough of them. Often, it was only one player, Pulisic. Lastly, we never had a consistently good team spirit, and our domestic players and players abroad were rarely on the same page. We lacked the ability of a typical US team to be consistently better than its parts. The 2002 team not only had more quality, but those players also had great camaraderie, which supported them to fight for ninety minutes in every game.

I need to accept the responsibility for this shortcoming, especially because of the technical deficiencies that we had. However, I tell you, it is a troubling trend. Modern-day athletes are delicate. Although blessed with some impressive athletic qualities, they often lack a strong mental approach to the game, and at times place themselves ahead of the team. These issues are constantly in the forefront in a national team program, and a coach often must work hard to get everyone on the same page. It takes time, patience, and experience to build a national team, and these requirements should be considered as US Soccer prepares to select the next national team coach.

We always knew we had a small margin for error in the World Cup qualifying campaign. After playing a total of fourteen games (friendlies, Gold Cup, World Cup qualifying) without losing, in the most important games at the end, we failed to produce the results necessary to go to Russia. The team's record for the year was ten wins, two losses, and six draws. We scored thirty-three goals and conceded thirteen. In World Cup Qualifying we had three wins, two losses, and three draws, scoring sixteen goals and conceding seven. In our last four games, we won once, drew once, and lost two critical games to Costa Rica and Trinidad and Tobago. In the end, we were a little shy of talent, a little unlucky, and crucially had a group of players who succumbed to the pressure on the critically important last day of our campaign. As one veteran texted me later, "Clearly things didn't end the way we would've liked them to. . . . Unfortunately we as players let you down."

In all fairness to all involved, the 2017 World Cup qualifying campaign was marred by a number of injuries, particularly to our backline. I felt that if we qualified for the World Cup in 2018, we would require multiple changes to the team that played against Trinidad and Tobago. Here would be my guess, keeping in mind, injuries, form, etc., and the fact that we would have close to a month of training together as a team beforehand to prepare for the opening game of the World Cup. I believe we might have made as many as six changes to our first eleven.

And of course, some of our young, emerging players—such as Paul Arriola, Tyler Adams, Weston McKennie, and Cristian Roldan—would have been strong candidates to make our final twenty-three-man roster, which would likely have included Tim Howard, Clint Dempsey, and Darlington Nagbe, among others.

G
Brad Guzan

D   **D**   **D**   **D**
DeAndre Yedlin   Matt Miazga   John Brooks   Jorge Villafaña

M   **M**
Kellyn Acosta   Michael Bradley

M   **M**
Sebastian Lletget   Christian Pulisic

M   **M**
Jordan Morris   Jozy Altidore

Our talent base of players needs to improve greatly in our next cycle. We have not developed more than one or two high-quality players in our country, and I don't believe we will have many US footballers in Europe who will be playing on a regular basis at a high level. Therefore, we need to find a way to get more young Americans on the field in Major League Soccer, so as to develop them into quality players. I shared these thoughts with Landon Donovan, and he agreed with me. There is no easy solution, and everything can't be on MLS alone. Coaching at all levels can improve—youth, amateur, and professional. Our black hole for our players is between the ages of seventeen and twenty-one. Currently, we have not created a good enough daily environment for these players, and this is clearly one of our big challenges. This is a huge task, and I believe that this will require a strong collaborative effort on part of US Soccer and Major League Soccer. Our ability to compete well at the international level on a consistent basis will require that our domestic league (MLS) and other domestic soccer programs revamp themselves so as to develop the American player. That's clearly the solution to the "American problem."

MLS and US Soccer

Major League Soccer plays the biggest role in developing elite players in the United States. With few exceptions, its academy programs consist of our top American youth players, so let's look at their technical department.

Hate to tell you this: there isn't a full-fledged technical department. They do hire outside consultants, such as Double Pass from Belgium, to evaluate their clubs, and they do hire the French Football Federation to educate their academy directors.

From what I have seen over the years, there has been some merit in outsourcing some soccer development, but I also think that it's time that MLS and US Soccer take on the responsibility of evaluating and training their clubs and academy directors. We a have a unique environment in our sport, and we can't just copy the models in Europe. We need to solve the "American problem" with American ideas and with mostly American people. Keep in mind that any good ideas we may have will work only if we have good people in charge. Clearly this will be a great challenge that will truly test our soccer culture. It is time that MLS and US Soccer step forward and take strong leadership and management roles in solving the "American problem."

In all fairness, the league has had a functioning technical committee, which is composed primarily of head coaches and technical/sporting directors. They send recommendations to the league's Product Strategy Committee (PSG), which will pass on recommendations to the Board of Governors (whose members represent the owners). This technical committee addresses issues like playoff formats, scheduling, disciplinary decisions, and other so-called technical issues. The PSG also deals with a lot of the financial issues associated with building rosters, salary caps, TAM, etc., and it is the committee that has the most influence on decision making.

Unfortunately, I'm not sure that there's a good understanding there of the day-to-day issues that have an impact on the technical side of what happens on the field. This negatively affects the product on the field. Understanding at the top of the technical challenges faced by players and staff needs to improve if we want to develop a top-flight professional league. Do we have the proper facilities, coaching, and administrative/managerial staffs—and the proper goals and philosophies—at each club? Is there an understanding as to how to coordinate the academy program with the second team and both with the first team? Are the programs at our clubs developing our young players? Do we have the proper rules and regulations in place to support the programs we have developed? Do we have senior people in management who understand these issues and can mentor and guide the clubs?

When the MLS started, in 1996, part of its charge was to develop American players, thus improving the US national team. After twenty-two years of existence, the mandate to develop players is even greater, but I don't believe we fully understand the issues and responsibility it takes to accomplish these goals.

Go back to my example of starting players in the 2017 MLS playoffs who would be eligible to play for the US National Team. This pool is shrinking, and very few of our young players are being developed or playing on the first teams of their MLS clubs.

An increasing number of international players of all ages have entered the league. Is the major focus of the league to improve the product on the field, something that will lead to better television packages and sponsorships? Do we have a real interest in developing the American player? As is the case in other countries, we have divergent visions between our professional league (MLS) and our federation (US Soccer). While the professional league focuses on the commercial side of the business—in growth and revenue and profitability—the federation should concentrate on developing the game and players. Finding the proper balance between these leading soccer entities in our country is our challenge.

Today in MLS it is clear that the growing presence of international players is having an impact on developing American players. The number of international slots has increased, green cards are easily accessible and TAM (targeted allocation money) and GAM (general allocation money) have been used largely on international players, who now make up about half of the players in MLS. The average age of a starting American player has risen, and fewer younger players see any significant playing time in the league.

In 2017, US Soccer granted MLS 176 international slots (an average of eight per team). These slots can also be traded among the clubs. From what I'm told, US labor law mandates that green-card holders count as domestic players. Consequently, some teams carry a majority of international players on their senior rosters, and this minimizes opportunities for American players. At some clubs, as many as sixteen international players occupy team rosters.

It is time for our governing body, US Soccer, to take a proactive stand to help create better opportunities for the domestic players in Major League Soccer. It can mandate the number of international players who are eligible to play in the league by reducing the number of international slots. This number has been increased over time, but now it is time to reduce it. Also, new rules could require that a certain number of US passport holders are required to be in starting lineups and/or on game-day rosters. We just need to have the leadership and smarts to get this kind of stuff done.

The Mexican Federation passed a strict rule that defines how players can be classified as domestic players in Liga MX. Basically, he must have had a Mexican passport by the age of nineteen. This rule was put in place because of the increasing number of South American players who were becoming naturalized Mexican citizens in two years' time in accordance with Mexican migration law. Therefore, a player like US national team player Omar Gonzalez, who secured a Mexican passport at twenty-six years old, now counts as a foreign player in Liga MX.

In 2016, Liga MX announced the 10/8 rule, which limits the number of foreign-born players allowed in each match-day squad to ten and reserves eight spots for Mexican nationals. The league's defense of this rule was simple, it guaranteed eight home-grown Mexican players would be in each eighteen-player match-day squad, whereas in previous years this was not the case for a number of clubs. This rule has now been adjusted to be the 9/9 rule, which gives the Mexican player more opportunities and guarantees that two Mexican players will start in every game.

Despite these changes, there continue to be concerns in Mexico. In 2017, there was a majority of Mexican starters in the league, yet not many young players. The average Mexican starter was 27.3 years old, and fewer players were in attacking roles. "There is a clear disconnect between good youth development work at the U17 and U20 levels and players making the jump up," Tom Marshall wrote in a July 2016 article for ESPN FC. "These players can compete with other countries at youth national team tournaments but somewhere along the line, there is stagnation." In other words: expect more changes in Liga MX.

In 2017, England won the U-17 and U-20 World Championships, and the Football Association (FA) has set winning the 2022 World Cup as a major goal for English football. Credit for this progress has been attributed to their "homegrown player rule," which is designed to require clubs to develop young talent. The rule is far from perfect and will be tweaked to eventually get more young English players on the field and accelerate their development.

Greg Dyke, chairman of the FA, has been pushing for additional changes in the rules, calling for the number of required homegrown players in a top-flight twenty-five-man first-team squad to change to twelve from the current eight. As is the case in MLS, a homegrown player can be an international. However, it is clear that the FA is driving home the importance of the academy programs, with the goal of developing more young English players. In return, they believe this will improve their national team's chances at the 2022 World Cup.

Every country is unique, and it is the charge of leadership to develop programs that will satisfy the goals and visions of each national soccer culture. This requires strong leadership, a good plan, and good people. We are all disappointed not to be a part of the 2018 World Cup. I hope we have learned some lessons and can move forward to make sure such a letdown does not happen again. Can we one day hold up the World Cup Trophy? I think so.

Checklist

It's time to get to work to make the changes soccer needs in this country, as we begin the task of repositioning our country to be a global leader in the sport. Let me conclude with a list of priority items for the short term, if we want to improve our sport and continue to develop the American player.

US SOCCER
1. Support the new president, Carlos Cordeiro.
2. Get chosen to host 2026 World Cup.
3. Hire a general manager for the national team.
4. Form a technical department and hire a technical director.
5. Hire a national team coach.
6. Modify MLS international player rules to foster development of domestic players.
7. Consider promotion and relegation in division-two and division-three leagues.

MLS
1. Hire a senior manager with "technical responsibilities."
2. Form a technical department and hire a technical director.
3. Slow down expansion.

4. Create policies to play more domestic players.
5. Create a better environment in the academy programs and on second teams.
6. Lengthen the regular season and shorten the playoffs.
7. Work toward a more balanced regular-season schedule.

Acknowledgments

My first full-time job in coaching began in 1978 at the University of Virginia, and it's an honor to still be involved in the game forty years later. I am thankful to my parents (Vincent and Adeline), my brothers (Paul and Mike), and twin sister (Barbara), who raised me to have a value system and to be tough and disciplined, and who simply tolerated my youthful mischiefs.

As a youngster and young man, sports became my world. I looked forward to the next game to play, the next ball to master, or the next challenge as I tested my skills in baseball, football, wrestling, lacrosse, and soccer. I knew nothing else, and my life could not have been any better. I enjoyed tagging along with my brothers as they ventured into their sporting interests—football and lacrosse. I looked up to them and wanted to follow in their footsteps. However, I had a mind of my own and chased my own sporting interests along the way, and this journey led me to cross the paths of some great coaches and people—and the sport of soccer. Ultimately, coaching would be my profession and a big part of my life. My journey has allowed me to meet so many incredible people—my players, my coaches, my administrators, my bosses, the fans, my competitors, my friends, and a great number of leaders and dignitaries (imagine, this kid from Long Island has met presidents and world leaders!). I'm a very fortunate person and I'm very thankful.

The book gives the reader insight on my evolution in becoming a coach. Coaching is a tough business, and coaches can be very selfish people. At times, we spend more time with other people and their families than our very own. My son, Kenny, grew up without a father on most weekends during his childhood as I chased my dream of becoming a coach. My wife, Phyllis, has been at my side the entire time and rarely complained. Looking back, I deeply appreciate the role my son and wife have played in my life. They allowed me to chase my dream, and I am indebted to them and love them very much.

A special thanks to everyone at HarperCollins, especially my editor, Luke Dempsey, a passionate soccer fan and author of *Club Soccer 101*. My friend and longtime agent, Richard Motzkin, has been a great confidant and sounding board for me for the past twenty years. He has been an incredible person to have worked with in our profession and in life. Being a novice in writing a book, I was extremely fortunate to have Steve Kettmann as my partner. I could never have undertaken this project without Steve's help. He's a tremendous writer, with many bestsellers to his credit, and I'm extremely grateful for his insight and guidance.

Finally, I'd like to thank every coach and every player I've worked with along the way; you learn from everyone and gain a better sense of what's important. I've always been fortunate to be surrounded with very good people who often made me look better than I was. I've had the privilege to work with many great players, great coaches, and great people throughout my career, and in all honesty, I could fill many pages with all the people I should thank by name and credit for helping me in my career. Suffice it to say, I've been a very lucky person and have had incredible experiences. I'm extremely grateful for all the wonderful people who have played such important roles in the successes that have come my way.

About the Author

Bruce Arena is the winningest coach in US soccer history. As head coach at the University of Virginia, he led the Cavaliers to five ACC Tournament Championships and five National Championships. Arena first became the head coach of the US Men's National Team in 1998, is the first coach in history to win three CONCACAF Gold Cups, and has coached teams to five MLS Cup championships. A member of the National Soccer Hall of Fame, Arena has thrice been named the MLS Coach of the Year, and in 2014 he received the Werner Fricker Builder Award, the highest honor that an individual can receive from the US Soccer Federation.